The Economics of Codetermination

The Economics of Codetermination

Lessons from the German Experience

John T. Addison

THE ECONOMICS OF CODETERMINATION
Copyright © John T. Addison, 2009.

All rights reserved.

First published in 2009 by
PALGRAVE MACMILLAN®
in the United States—a division of St. Martin's Press LLC,
175 Fifth Avenue, New York, NY 10010.

Where this book is distributed in the UK, Europe and the rest of the world,
this is by Palgrave Macmillan, a division of Macmillan Publishers Limited,
registered in England, company number 785998, of Houndmills,
Basingstoke, Hampshire RG21 6XS.

Palgrave Macmillan is the global academic imprint of the above companies
and has companies and representatives throughout the world.

Palgrave® and Macmillan® are registered trademarks in the United States,
the United Kingdom, Europe and other countries.

ISBN: 978–0–230–60609–8

Library of Congress Cataloging-in-Publication Data

Addison, John T.
    The economics of codetermination : lessons from the German
    experience / John T. Addison.
        p. cm.
    Includes bibliographical references and index.
    ISBN 978–0–230–60609–8
        1. Management—Employee participation. I. Title.

HD5650.A313 2009
338.6′9—dc22   2009006871

A catalogue record of the book is available from the British Library.

Design by Newgen Imaging Systems (P) Ltd., Chennai, India.

First edition: November 2009

10 9 8 7 6 5 4 3 2 1

Printed in the United States of America.

Contents

Tables

Preface

The origins of this book date back to my first publication on works councils a little more than 15 years ago. The attraction of works councils to an uprooted British labor economist working in the United States and at that time allocating a still significant part of his research effort to the economics of trade unions was powerful. In the first place, the theory and practice of works councils offered a much improved milieu for the study of *collective voice* than the entity and country for which that model was first developed—unions in the United States. More practically, the headlong retreat of unionism at least in the U.S. private sector threatened to transform what had been a fairly dynamic Anglo-Saxon research area into a near pathology.

Over the years, with the steady improvement in data sets, documented here, the economic analysis of German codetermination was to flourish. Of course, research on works councils predates the attentions of economists, and indeed had long been the preserve of sociologists. They have undertaken important work on works councils and at times must have cringed at the early efforts of economists. Nevertheless, their work is little mentioned in the present text, not out of criticism but simply because there has been an explosion of interest by economists in the subject. It is now time to take stock of the progress *we* have made, and that is the aim of the present text.

The next few years will open up new questions that will exercise economists and other social scientists alike. A more integrative treatment might well be appropriate at that time with the challenge of globalization to the labor movement, the dual system, and corporate governance alike. There will be much to study and how well German institutions adapt to heightened regime competition should be of interest to us all. As I have implied, it may even bring sometimes uneasy bedfellows together. Some protean lines of future inquiry are sketched in this treatment.

In writing this book, I owe a heavy debt of gratitude to individuals and institutions.

To those fellow Europeans with whom I have worked on journal articles on *Mitbestimmung*, I clearly owe most of all. This book would simply have proved impossible to write without the contributions of Joachim Wagner, Claus Schnabel, Lutz Bellmann, Paulino Teixeira, Thorsten Schank, Thomas Zwick, Arnd Kölling, and Kornelius Kraft. I have further to thank, without implicating, my friend Claus Schnabel for reading and commenting on every single chapter. Thanks are also due to Stefan Zagelmeyer who though sorely pressed found the time to comment on chapter 8. In short, I could not ask for better collaborators and colleagues.

I have to thank institutions, too. Chief among these are the Moore School of Business at the University of South Carolina and Queen's University Management School Belfast. I thank them for providing me with a first-class research environment. The Moore School's Center for International Business Education and Research also funded several trips to Germany that permitted material progress to be made on the original research underpinning several chapters in this book. I am also happy to acknowledge the facilitating role of the Institute for Employment Research of the German Federal Employment Agency where I have spent much productive and stimulating time as Research Fellow over the past few years. To them all, my hearty thanks.

CHAPTER 1

Introduction

This book examines employee involvement through representative agencies. It is less concerned, then, with direct participation other than in relation to representative participation. And since the focus is squarely upon German codetermination, or *Mitbestimmung* (literally, having a voice in), it is less concerned with that other form of representative involvement—unionism—than with works councils at establishment level and board level representation at company or enterprise level. That said, although works councils are formally independent of unions the links are in practice close because (in no particular order of importance) works councils are embedded within the dual system of industrial relations in Germany, most works councilors are union members, and union nominees sit alongside employee workplace representatives on company boards. It follows that the union-codetermination nexus cannot be ignored.

The German system of codetermination is more extensive than in any other European nation. But note that the notion that the interests of employees be formally and systematically recognized under law is by no means alien to the European tradition. Indeed, in this regard the German system is often viewed as an exemplar of participative practice. Thus, when it comes to policy formation in the European Union, Germany has often been regarded as a first-pass template for European-wide mandates. And latterly measures to increase the involvement of employees in their companies have occupied center-stage in the EU social space, the most pertinent recent example being national systems for informing and consulting workers. That said, there is little external appeal in the German system of board representation and, at this level, Germany will likely increasingly have to accommodate itself to a certain convergence of company law and to mandates from without.

Notwithstanding the union-codetermination nexus, the German experience also has external relevance because of the headlong retreat of unionism in many countries. Recognizing the benefits to workplace governance and contract execution associated with unions, might not new institutions akin to the works council fill the representation gap? More to the point, might not works councils be advantageous in such countries, especially if they offer the prospect of detaching production issues from questions of distribution? It follows that quite apart from its intrinsic interest, German codetermination is of wider concern.

Mitbestimmung in Germany has a long history and has been the subject of considerable economic investigation. Even so, economic issues have received comparatively minor attention in the public policy debate in that country that has been more preoccupied with notions of industrial democracy/democratic deficits and issues of fairness. Our concern is to redress the imbalance by bringing economic issues to the forefront. This is because commentators impressed with the ideas that codetermination fosters a well-functioning social democracy and helps to prevent divisions in society have taken it as read that what is good for social cohesion and industrial relations is necessarily good for economic success. Is this the case?

To this end, having set the scene by outlining the long history of codetermination (legislation dates back to 1920 and its antecedents to 1848), including the most recent changes to the Works Constitution Act, we will examine the theory of and evidence pertaining to codetermination. For its part, the theory is by no means inimical to the German institution(s), although there are grounds for differentiating between works councils on the one hand and worker directors on the other. We will examine the arguments for and against both institutions, paying especial attention to the themes of property rights, contract theory, transaction costs, collective voice, and rent seeking. We will also discuss the possibility that otherwise beneficial codetermination arrangements might be underprovided by the market. This will lead in turn to the discussion of the potentially pivotal role of institutional rules such as the "peace obligation" imposed on works councils as well as union agreements that might hold the distributive aspects of works councils in check.

Since theory does not offer definitive guidance, much of the balance of our discussion is given over to setting down carefully what is known (and what is *not* known) of the consequences of works councils *and* board membership for firm performance. Perforce our discussion will also on occasion involve that other institution of the dual system, industry-wide collective bargaining.

Much of our review of the empirical evidence will apply to codetermination at establishment level (or *betriebliche Mitbestimmung*). No less than three chapters are dedicated to the evolving empirical evidence on works council impact. Interestingly, this evidence follows a sequence quite the reverse of that characterizing U.S. research into union impact. That is to say, early German studies pointed unequivocally to adverse effects of works councils on firm performance. With the emergence of larger data sets, a more nuanced interpretation of works council impact became more commonplace. Next, the availability of nationally representative data sets produced some truly revisionist work, including the result that works council presence was associated with a positive productivity effect of around 30 percent (and as such very close to the initial U.S. estimates of union impact; see Brown and Medoff, 1978). This particular result now seems contraindicated by more recent findings based on panel analyses, matching models, and quantile regressions. A more balanced modern view, then, is that excessive revulsion against the institution (evident in the very early literature) is just as misplaced as euphoria (surrounding some of the more recent estimates).

Our review of this part of the empirical literature covers all aspects of firm performance: productivity, profitability, investments in physical and intangible capital, employment growth (including plant failures), labor turnover, training, wages and the wage distribution, and organizational flexibility. Some key themes examined are the interaction between works councils and collective bargaining proper and, given that the overall effect of works councils is likely to be small, on the role of factors that might produce shifts around this average relation. One of our conclusions is that future research should examine the role of the quality of the works council and/or the state of labor relations at the plant. Another is the need to model the interaction between works councils and high performance work practices.

Next we consider the effects of codetermination at the company or enterprise level (*Unternehmensmitbestimmung*). What has been learned of the effects on firm performance of worker representation on company boards? Not surprisingly, the evidence is much thinner than for works councils at establishment level and is largely limited to analyses of differences in the degree of codetermination. Among other things, we shall examine events studies of the 1976 extension of (quasi-)parity board representation beyond the coal and steel sector. That is, we review studies examining stock market reactions to the effect of court decisions on whether the more extensive codetermination rules should apply to a firm as well as more conventional before-and-after regression studies of a given firm's productivity and return on equity. In addition, and among other things, we shall also look at financial studies that compare firms with quasi-parity representation on company boards to firms with one-third representation (and no representation) using pooled time-series cross-section data for a variety of rate of return variables. On net, the modern literature tends to point to a more sanguine view of the efficacy of board representation than recent characterizations of *Unternehmensmitbestimmung* by employers might indicate—subject that is to potentially crucially important caveats concerning the extent of representation and the role of union nominees. But this may not stand in the way of an erosion of quasi-parity representation in the wake of other developments, even if public support for worker directors may well have grown with the perception that codetermination limits the influence of strategic financial investors (presumably to include Franz Müntefering's "locusts") on corporate management.

Our attention turns in the penultimate chapter to EU preoccupations; in particular, the web of rules surrounding the employers' duty to inform and consult workers. We refer here to the provisions implicit in the plethora of health and safety directives, the directives on collective redundancies, transfers of business/takeovers, European Works Councils, the worker involvement provisions of the European Company Stature, and legislation establishing a general framework for informing and consulting employees. We implicitly examine the pedigree of such measures. This exercise will also involve an assessment of the influence of German institutions on Europe and European institutions on Germany.

Finally, we review *Mitbestimmung* in retrospect and prospect. The retrospective component largely draws together the threads of the preceding economic analysis. As far as future prospects are concerned, these hinge partly on the health of the German union movement, whose decline has implications for the dual system as whole. Politically, no further changes in the national legislative framework are likely. The innovations that occur are likely to be driven by globalization and EU developments. Some changes in company codetermination are likely. Whether a codetermination deficit emerges in the wake of any decline in works council frequency and coverage depends on the extent of alternative forms of worker involvement (including "fair share capitalism" and teamwork) and growth in alternative institutional forms of worker representation. Works councils might even grow in importance in view of transnational works councils on the one hand and on the other by reason of their involvement in negotiations over the shape of worker representative bodies in the new European Companies and as a result of changes in company law.

CHAPTER 2

Context: What Is Codetermination?

2.1 Introduction

The goal of codetermination or *Mitbestimmung* is the resolution of conflict through dialogue rather than force. German codetermination seeks to guarantee employee involvement in the regulation of working conditions as well as in economic planning and decision making. *Mitbestimmung* is based on notions of equality of capital and labor, considerations of industrial democracy, and the need for stability through social development, and coresponsibility. It takes place at two levels: at the establishment through the agency of the works council (or *Betriebsrat*) and at enterprise level through company codetermination (*Unternehmensmitbestimmung*). Codetermination is one of the special features of so-called *Rhenish* capitalism with its emphasis on collective, long-run success and a guided or coordinated market economy.[1]

In this chapter, we trace the development of both forms of codetermination, beginning with the workplace level, to the present day. We conclude with a statement as to the status quo ante and the extent of codetermination.

2.2 History

2.2.1 Representation through the Works Council

The rights of the works council are laid down in the 2001 Work Constitution Act as amended by the Art. 81 Law of December 23, 2003 (see below). But the history of codetermination at the workplace dates back to World War I with the formation of workers' committees (*Arbeiterausschüsse*) to mobilize support for the war effort in plants essential to that end.[2] The committees set up in establishments with over 50 employees in 1916—under the *Gesetz über den Vaterländischen*

Hilfsdient—had consultation rights rather than codetermination powers per se but were accompanied by conciliation bodies to settle workplace disagreement. (The immediate precursors of these joint factory committees were the largely advisory worker councils established under Bavarian and Prussian mining laws [or *Bergwerkgesetze*] in 1900 and 1905 for operations with more than 20 and 100 workers, respectively, to administer safety rules and cooperate with management in improving productivity.)

The wartime factory committees were transformed into works councils in establishments with more than 20 workers under the 1920 Works Councils Act of February 4, 1920. This *Betriebsrätegesetz*, itself facilitated by the 1919 Weimar Constitution (Art. 165), largely set the format of present-day workplace codetermination. The Act provided for full codetermination rights in the determination of workplace regulations and participation rights in a variety of personnel and finance matters. In view of subsequent innovations, note that the committees at this time were to be distinctly subordinate to trade unions who were not only to be given the right to advise them but also the right to set up collectively bargained alternatives. Note, too, that the 1920 legislation also prepared the way for employee representation on the supervisory boards of companies (see subsection 2.2.2, below).

The backdrop to the 1920 law was threatened revolution in the aftermath of the war. As described by Thelen (1991) and Brigl-Matthiaβ (1978), the political goal was to marginalize the splinter revolutionary works council movement of the communists and independent socialists. Legislation that strengthened the shop-floor power of mainstream unions but did not fundamentally challenge capital was in the first instance accepted by employers because of the more unpalatable revolutionary alternative. The bottom line is that works councils at this time were the creatures of the (reformist) unions.

But the situation was shortly to change. First of all, the economic crisis of the 1920s systematically eroded works council influence as employers sought to restore management prerogative. Second, in line with the *Führerprinzip* the National Socialist government dismantled at a stroke the "divisive" industrial relations apparatus. For their part, unions were simply absorbed within the Labor Front (*Deutsche Arbeitsfront*), a unitary organization embracing a "social community" of labor and capital. Works councils were replaced by "committees of trusted men" to advise management on production and personnel matters. Under the Act to Regulate National Work (*Gesetz zur Ordnung der nationalen Arbeit*), the enabling legislation of 1920 was repealed (and the related provisions for worker representation at board level expunged). Following World War II, works councils sprang up in an attempt to build unions "from the bottom up" (Thelen, 1991, p. 72). Informal and sometimes far-reaching arrangements at plant level were subsequently formalized under laws in individual *Länder*. In this endeavor, the parties were supported by the labor policy of the occupying powers, geared to promoting strong ties between union and works council. Of the two pieces of Allied legislation, one related to works councils and the other to board membership (discussed in the next subsection). The former mandate was Allied Law No. 22 (*Das Kontrollratsgesetz Nr. 22*). This fiat of April 10, 1946, was based on the German legislation of 1920 and it sought to standardize the rules on the establishment and role of plant councils. As noted, it was explicit in requiring councils to operate in collaboration with recognized unions.

Following the establishment of the Federal Republic, German law succeeded Allied mandates. In October 1952 the Works Constitution Act (*Betriebsverfassungsgesetz*), codifying the rights and responsibilities of works councils, entered the statute books. It conveyed fewer rights than some of the now superseded state legislation and for this reason is widely characterized as a "defeat" for organized labor.

The 1952 Act still forms much of the basis of the information, consultation, and codetermination rights of works councils that will be presented in detail below. For present purposes, three themes of the legislation might usefully be identified here. First, the Act now emphasized the independence of the works council from the union, and indeed recognized only limited rights for unions in the plant. Second, the works council was enjoined to work together with the employer in a "spirit of mutual trust." As part and parcel of their peace obligation, councils were now forbidden to undertake industrial action. Third, the Act sought to protect the representation rights of minorities and salaried workers through specific election rules.

The initial reaction of the union movement to these "setbacks" is described by Thelen in some detail (1991, pp. 78–81). One such response was to form shop stewards committees (*Vertrauensleutekörper*) to deal with the implied threat to union membership. Another was to "infiltrate" works councils. It was not until the early 1960s that suspicion of works councils subsided. By that time, with the centralization of wage bargaining, the works council was to become the union's preferred means of deflecting a challenge to its authority from below (p. 81).

The reforms sought by organized labor in response to the setbacks of 1952 came with the election of a Social Democratic (SPD) government in 1969, in coalition with the Free Democrats, or FDP. The principal changes introduced under the new administration's 1972 Works Constitution Act were threefold. First, the information and consultation rights of the works council were materially extended in respect of management decisions that might involve major changes in capacity, working operations, and production processes, inter alia. Further, employers now had a duty to bargain with the works council over compensation for any resulting mass layoffs. Second, the legislation significantly strengthened the existing codetermination rights of works councils by (1) extending them and (2) providing for their adjudication in the event of impasse. Both developments increased the bargaining power of the works council. Third, although the formal independence of works councils was maintained, the access of unions to the workplace was improved (e.g., the right to attend meetings between management and the works council) and they could require the works council to hold works meetings. Rather more important, the unions could now submit lists of candidates in works council elections without having to meet the initial support levels set for other groups, while works councilors could simultaneously hold union office (e.g., serve on bargaining committees) and attend union training courses.

We are almost at the end of the legislative innovations. But there was to be one further change.[3] A new Works Constitution Act (*BetrVerf-Reformgesetz*) became effective on July 28, 2001. The immediate backdrop to the legislation is provided by the deliberations of a codetermination commission (*Kommission Mitbestimmung*) and the debate pursuant to its conclusions (see Addison, Bellmann, Schnabel, and Wagner, 2004). Among other things, the *Kommission* was set up to evaluate experience with the workings of the 1972 Act. It comprised high-ranking scientific, economic, union, and political representatives, and was supported by expert reports from the academic community. The *Kommission's* final report, entitled *Co-Determination and New Business Cultures— Conclusion and Perspectives*, was presented in May 1998 (*Kommission Mitbestimmung*, 1998). It reasoned that it cannot be decided from either theory or the [extant] empirical evidence whether the overall effect of works councils is positive or negative: "In the real world codetermination as an institution generates both efficiency-reducing misallocation and efficiency-raising productivity and cooperative effects. The net impact of these parallel and simultaneous partial effects cannot be determined *a priori*" (English translation, para. 27; *Kommission*

Mitbestimmung, 1998, paras. 5.22–5.23, pp. 64–65). Although the commission did not offer any concrete proposals for the reform of existing legislation—rather, it elaborates 26 recommendations for the future design of German codetermination based on joint initiatives from social partners (i.e., the two sides of industry)—it does emphasize the presence of a large and growing codetermination-free zone (see below) warning that "A gradual erosion [of the institution of codetermination] cannot, in the public interest, be left to the vagaries of the market" (*Kommission Mitbestimmung*, 1998, para. 6.16, p. 76).

The (eventual) response of the Social Democrat-Green coalition government (elected in the Fall of 1998) was to be accommodating, seeking to stimulate works council formation. The main changes it introduced were as follows. First, the structure of the works council became more diverse than heretofore. In enterprises with more than one establishment, works councils could now be formed across some or all of the constituent establishments, while for enterprises that were organized along "lines of business" it might follow the self-same divisional structure. Second, the creation of a works council was to be facilitated in establishments employing between 5 and 50 employees through a simplified voting procedure.[4] (The traditional procedure is outlined in Addison, Schnabel, and Wagner, 2000a). This procedure could also be extended to establishments with 51–100 employees with the agreement of management. Third, the thresholds used to determine the size of the works council were lowered. (For example, the number of works councilors in an establishment with 150 employees was raised from 5 to 7 and in an establishment with 500 employees from 9 to 11). Fourth, employers were required to make provision for a full-time works councilor in establishments with 200 or more employees, instead of 300 as before. Fifth, the thresholds for additional full-time councilors were also lowered. Sixth, the employer had to furnish the works council at his/her own expense with modern information and communication equipment. Seventh, the influence of the works council in matters of employment protection and the training of the workforce was strengthened, including the possibility of enforcing training measures benefiting employees whose qualifications had been rendered obsolete. Also, the works council was ceded codetermination rights in the execution of teamwork. Eighth, codetermination on environmental protection issues was explicitly recognized as a function of the works council. Ninth, gender equality was facilitated by the requirement that the minority gender at the establishment be represented on the works council at least in proportion to its employment share. Finally, the works council was given the formal means to avoid racial discrimination at the workplace via its power to withhold consent in matters of the engagement and transfer of personnel in special cases (see Addison, Bellmann, Schnabel, and Wagner, 2004).

These amendments to the Works Constitution Act were introduced in the face of a decline in works council coverage (if not a decline in worker participation per se). As we shall report, they do not appear to have led to a growth in either the frequency or coverage of the institution.

2.2.2 Representation through Membership on Company Boards

Even at a descriptive level it is impossible to divorce *Unternehmensmitbestimmung*, or company codetermination, from *betriebliche Mitbestimmung* because the laws providing for the latter have also contained rules covering the latter. Sometimes the links have been more direct. So it was that a 1922 Act first provided for the representation of works council members on the supervisory or administrative boards of companies. Specifically, the Act allowed for two works council members with full voting rights in joint stock companies and for one works council member in smaller companies.

The next legal development was seemingly from without. Under an agreement between the trust administration of the iron and steel producing industry in the British Zone of Occupation and the trade unions specific provision was made for equal board membership. In fact, "from without" is a misnomer since unions won significant concessions from management either as a result of the immediate postwar power vacuum in the Ruhr or as a consequence of voluntary alliances where management embraced unions fearing the dismantlement/permanent foreign control of industrial plant. In short, the law was essentially ring-holding prior to the formation of a German government.

Subsequent developments in codetermination at enterprise level therefore codified matters in the new Federal Republic under the April 1951 Act on the Codetermination of Employees in the Supervisory and Management Boards of Companies in the Coal, Iron and Steel Industry (*Gesetz über die Mitbestimmung der Arbeitnehmer in den Aufsichtsräten und Vorständen der Unternehmen des Bergbaus und der Eisen und Stahl erzeugenden Industrie*). This *Montan-Mitbestimmungsgesetz*, as it is also known, ceded full-parity codetermination in such sector-specific companies generally employing over 1,000 workers. Specifically, it established supervisory boards ranging in size from 11 to 21 members, according to share capital, comprising equal numbers of shareholder and worker members (strictly speaking one or more members of each side—according to the size of the board—is an "additional" member) and one neutral member. Further, the appointment of a Labor Director, who serves on the management board, required the agreement of the employee representatives. Two further main enactments sought to protect *Montanmitbestimmung*. In 1956, the Supplementary Codetermination Act (*Mitbestimmungsergänzungsgesetz*) extended the scope of the Act to include parent companies that although they had no coal, iron, or steel operations of their own nonetheless controlled subsidiaries active in that sector contributing at least 50 percent of the added value of the concern. In 1989 a further amendment lowered this contribution to net output to 20 percent, or circumstances in which the subsidiaries employed more than 2,000 employees. If they had previously accepted the participation of workers in the supervisory bodies of the sector, the new laws were to attract strong opposition from employer groups (see below).

The 1952 Works Constitution Act (see above) generalized worker directors. Unlike the situation in coal, iron, and steel, however, the law provided for a weaker form of codetermination. Basically it provided for one-third representation of employees on the supervisory boards of large and medium-sized corporations with more than 500 employees. The specifics of the Act were as follows. Employees were to have one-third representation on the supervisory boards of joint stock corporations (*Aktiengesellschaften*, AGs) and partnerships limited by shares (*Kommanditgesellschaften auf Aktien*, KGaAs) with up to 2,000 employees. Family-owned companies with less than 500 employees were exempted from the Act. (More recently, to encourage mid-sized companies going public, joint stock corporations established after August 10, 1994, and employing fewer than 500 employees, were exempted from codetermination under the Act.) For their part, limited liability companies (*Gesellschaften mit beschränkter Haftung*, GmbHs) were covered by the Act if they had more than 500 employees.

In March 1976 under the Codetermination Act (*Mitbestimmungsgesetz*), provision for equal numbers of representatives from the employee side and the company side on the supervisory board was extended from the coal, iron, and steel industry to corporations in all other industries that employed (as a rule) more than 2,000 employees, either alone or taken as a whole with their subsidiaries.[5] The number of seats on the supervisory board was a function of employment size: 12 members if the employment total did not exceed 10,000, 16 if it exceeded 10,000 but fell below 20,000, and 20 where it was greater than 20,000. Election of the chairman and vice chairman of the supervisory board in each case required majorities of two-thirds of the votes. If neither gained the necessary votes, the shareholder (worker) representatives were to elect the chairman (vice chairman). This procedure ensured that the chairman was always a shareholder representative and he/she has an extra, tie-breaking vote unlike the situation the *Montan* industries. Hence the expression "quasi-parity" codetermination rather than the "full-parity" codetermination obtaining in iron, coal, and steel. The law also made provision for the inclusion of managerial employees, who were given one seat on the supervisory board. Finally, in this case the worker directors had no right of veto in respect of the appointment of the labor director.

The 1976 changes bring us almost up to date with respect to innovations in company level codetermination. The most recent change in the law was the so-called Third Part Act (*Drittelbeteiligungsgesetz*) of 2004. This legislation made minor amendments to the sections of the 1952 Works Constitution Act dealing with supervisory board membership in companies with 500–2,000 employees.

To summarize, the proportion of worker representatives on company boards varies from one-third, in companies with between 500 and 2,000 employees, to one-half, in companies with more than 2,000 workers. In the latter, the chair in effect represents the shareholders and has the casting vote. The exception is the larger coal or iron and steel companies where the chair is independent; implying full-parity representation. The number of members of the supervisory board is determined either by the share capital or employment of the company or group.[6]

We conclude with some brief observations on the role of the *Aufsichtsrat* or supervisory board on which workers are represented, and upon the controversy surrounding board representation in Germany (which is examined in greater detail in chapter 8). As far as the functions of the supervisory board are concerned, according to the 1965 Stock Corporation Act (*Aktiengesetz*), these are basically fourfold. It approves the appointment of members of the *Vorstand* or management board; it monitors the management board (which has to inform it of the broad lines of business policy and corporate planning on an annual basis and of business operations on a more regular basis); it can codetermine business operations requiring its approval; and it scrutinizes the annual accounts of the company or group. Note that although the worker directors actively collaborate with the works council and unions (and 80 percent of worker directors are members of unions affiliated with the German Federation of Trade Unions/*Deutscher Gewerkschaftsbund*) they are charged with a duty of care and confidentiality. A final remark is that there are clear inconsistencies in the existing system of board level representation. Perhaps the most obvious example here concerns reporting requirements; in particular, the management board in private limited companies (GmbHs) has less detailed reporting requirements in relation to the supervisory board than its counterpart in a public company (AG).

We noted earlier employer opposition to the 1976 Codetermination Act, without offering a practical example. In 1977 9 companies and 29 employers' associations challenged the constitutionality of the Act arguing that it infringed the membership and property rights of shareholders and challenged freedom of assembly and association (under Articles 14 and 12 of the German Basic Law or *Grundgesetz*). Further, in 1979 the employers challenged the criteria contained in the 1956 Supplementary Codetermination Act for extending full-parity codetermination to sectors whose links to coal, iron, and steel were tenuous, offending the sector-specific nature of the 1951 Act. In both cases the employers were unsuccessful. In the former case, the Constitutional Court (*Bundesverfassungsgericht*) ruled that the basic law did not ordain a particular economic order and the protection of property had to be seen in the light of social context and function. It further resisted the notion of conflict between codetermination and free collective bargaining. In the latter case, the Court effectively concluded that the value-added criterion if not the employment level criterion furnished sufficient substantiation.

In the light of this employer opposition (further examined in chapter 8) to company codetermination—if not workplace codetermination, at least up to the 2001 legislation—it should come as no surprise that a high-level government commission under the chairmanship of Professor Kurt Biedenkopf charged with investigating adaptation of the law governing parity representation to changed economic and social circumstances (i.e., with modernizing the 1976 Act) soon reached impasse.

This Biedenkopf Commission was made up of equal numbers of academics and employer and union representatives.[7] Unable to reach consensus, the (3) academics on the committee published their own report (Biedenkopf Commission, 2006; Hans Böckler Stiftung, 2007). The report saw no need for a fundamental revision of codetermination, which was viewed as having met the bill, as having satisfied the *noneconomic* goal of furthering industrial democracy. As regards the subordinate economic case, the commission observed that "after lengthy discussion of the observable economic effects of employee representation at board level, the academic members see no overall reason to place in doubt the positive forecast of the legislation of 1976, and to propose a fundamental revision of the legislation, let alone its repeal," concluding that codetermination at company level had strengthened the motivation and sense of responsibility of workers and fostered social harmony (Hans Böckler Stiftung, 2007, p. 3).[8]

The main recommendation was that existing legislation be made simpler and more flexible on the basis of negotiations between the two sides, proposing that the worker side encompass representatives of the works council, the union, and senior management according to their composition on the relevant board and that decisions be reached on the basis of a three-quarters majority (on this and other proposals, see chapter 8). The particular negotiating body structure envisaged by the commission not only ruled out union leadership but it could also result in unions being outvoted and, in certain circumstances, even excluded.

As we shall see, the employers rejected the report largely because they sought a reduction in worker representation to one-third as a default value in the negotiating process—whereas at the outset the chair of the commission emphasized that any recommendations would have to be based on current legislation. The employer side also disagreed with what it saw as the commission's Pollyanna stance on the economics of *Unternehmensmitbestimmung* (its effects on investment decisions, dividends, takeovers, and the like; on which, see chapter 7). And, as noted earlier, union resistance was mainly because of the very real possibility that they could lose representation as a result of the negotiating process, which they palpably sought to lead.[9]

2.3   The Status Quo

Having outlined the historical context, we now proceed to consider the status quo ante. For *betriebliche Mitbestimmung*, this requires us to "organize" the key present-day rights of the works council, and then more briefly to address issues of incidence and coverage of the institution (and potential alternatives). For *Unternehmensmitbestimmung*, since the relevant themes have been rehearsed earlier, our narrative can largely touch upon controversies that will be explored in later chapters.

2.3.1 The Works Council Institution[10]

Our opening remark should be that the current Works Constitution Act (WCA) of 2001 preserves the principles of collaboration set under previous legislation. Thus, the employer and the works council are enjoined in their joint conferences to "discuss the matters at issue with an earnest desire to reach agreement and make suggestions for settling their differences" (§ 74 (1) WCA). Further, works councils continue to be forbidden to strike and, together with the employer, to "refrain from activities that interfere with the operations or imperil the peace in the establishment" (§ 74 (2) WCA).

2.3.1.1 Establishment and Composition of the Works Council

A works council may be elected in all companies employing at least five permanent employees with voting rights, including three who are eligible (to be work councilors).[11] They are mandatory but not automatic bodies. The initiative for setting up a works council lies with the employees. Three employees with voting rights, or a trade union represented in the establishment, are needed to call for a works meeting to elect an electoral board (*Wahlvorstand*), which is then responsible for holding the election. Once elections are under way, the works council is a fait accompli. The works council is elected in secret ballot by the entire labor force with the exception of senior executives (*Leitende Angestellte*). (In firms with at least 10 managerial employees, an executives' committee may be elected pursuant to the 1988 Executive Committee Act [*Sprecherausschussgesetz*]. The executive committee is independent of the works council and has information and consultation rights only.) The basic electoral process is elaborate, with lists of candidates—submitted by employees with voting rights and trade unions represented in the establishment—and with winners elected on the basis of proportional representation (see, for example, Addison, Schnabel, and Wagner, 2000a). But we earlier noted that the 2001 amendments introduced simplified election procedures in smaller establishments (see note 4). A related change is that in undertakings where there is no works council, an existing central works council or group level works council[12] can directly set up an electoral board to supervise the election of a works council in an establishment under a so-called mentoring principle. As was also noted earlier, the new Act also provides for the formation of cross-plant and cross-company works councils. Finally, the regular term of office for a works council is four years. Regular elections for the works council are held some time between March 1 and May 31.

In terms of organization, works council meetings are normally held within working hours. The employer may only attend if invited; similarly, union representatives may be invited to attend in an advisory capacity with the concurrence of one-quarter of the members of the works council. Note that although unions are not formally represented on works councils, they are indirectly since most works councilors are union members; (67 percent in 1998 when union density stood at one-third). The frequency of these meetings is supposed to take account of the operational needs of the establishment. The employer and the works council meet at least once a month in joint conferences.

Expenses of the works council are borne by the employer, including elections, facilities, and release time. In the latter context, there are full-time as well as part-time works councilors. The number of full-timers ranges from 1 member (where there are 200–500 employees) to 12 where there are 9,001–10,000 employees—and thence by 1 member for each incremental 2,000 employees.[13] Releases may also be granted in the form of partial releases.

2.3.1.2 Information, Consultation, and Codetermination Rights of the Works Council

The rights of the works council are of utmost importance to our inquiry. They range from rights of information, through rights of consultation and cooperation, to rights of codetermination. As we shall see, there are also a number of other rights, such as veto rights and consent rights, to be slotted into this continuum.

Beginning with the employer's duty to disclose information, the employer has to provide the works council with "comprehensive information...in good time" to enable it to discharge its general duties, including the right to inspect the necessary documentation (§ 80 (2) WCA).[14] (Information disclosure is of course a prerequisite of all the specific consultation rights noted below.) Moreover, in plants with more than 100 permanent employees, a finance committee (*Wirtschaftsausschuss*) has to be set up. It is appointed (and removed) by the works council and consists of between three and seven members, one of whom must be a works councilor. It has very far-reaching rights of information (and consultation) as regards the economic and financial aspects of the establishment. It meets monthly with the employer and has the right to consult experts. The employer has to inform the finance committee in full and good time of the financial affairs of the firm and supply it with the relevant documentation. That information covers the economic and financial situation of the company, the production and marketing situation, and production and investment programs, as well as rationalization plans, new working methods, and transfers/amalgamations, inter alia (§ 106 (3) WCA). The finance committee is charged with informing the works council on all these matters.

Consultation rights for their part cover actions envisaged by management in matters relating to the structuring, organization, and design of jobs, where the employer has to consult the works council in good time on the actions contemplated, taking particular account of their impact on the nature of work and the resultant demands on employees so that the suggestions and objections on the part of the works council can be taken into account in the plans (§ 90 (2) WCA). Consultation rights also figure largely in the area of manpower planning (§ 92 (1) WCA), where the works council may also make recommendations on the introduction and implementation of particular measures (§ 92 (2) WCA). In companies with more than 20 employees with voting rights, the employer has to consult the works council in advance of any new employment (§ 99 (1) WCA). The works council must also be consulted on individual dismissals (§ 102 (1) WCA); failure to consult in theses circumstances renders the dismissals null and void (see below).

In addition, apart from the consultation involved under Section 90, in companies that have 21 or more employees with voting rights, the employer has to inform the works council on proposed "alterations" that "may entail substantial prejudice to the staff or a large sector thereof" and consult it (section 111 WCA).[15] Such alterations include a reduction in operations in or closure/transfer of the whole or important departments of the establishment, amalgamation with other establishments, important changes in the organization, purpose or plant of the establishment, and the introduction of entirely new work methods and production processes. In such circumstances, as we shall see, the rights of the works council extend beyond consultation to encompass the negotiation of social (compensation) plans.

The works council has codetermination rights in so-called social matters, unless these are otherwise prescribed by collective agreement or legislation (§ 87 (1) WCA). Examples include such important matters as the rules of operation of the establishment, working hours (including short time and overtime working), holiday arrangements and their application, the deployment of techniques for monitoring the behavior and performance of workers, principles of remuneration and the introduction and application of new pay methods (or the modification of existing schemes), the fixing of job, bonus, and piece rates, and the principles governing the performance of teamwork, if not its introduction.

Additional codetermination rights cover accident prevention rules, the allocation of company-owned housing, and the administration of social services provided at plant level.

In all such comanagement areas the employer cannot act without the formal agreement of the works council. Failure to reach agreement leads to adjudication through a conciliation panel (*Einigungstelle*), comprising an equal number of employer- and works-council-nominated members plus an independent chairman.[16]

In addition, the works council has a set of "consent rights" covering guidelines for the selection of employees for recruitment, transfer, and dismissal and individual dismissals. The guidelines require the approval of the works council (§ 95 (1) WCA).[17] If no agreement is reached on the guidelines or their contents, the employer can apply to the conciliation committee for a decision, which then takes the place of an agreement between the employer and the works council.

As noted earlier, the works council must be consulted before every dismissal. Abstracting from exceptional dismissals, if the works council has objections to the dismissal it has to inform the employer in writing within one week, giving its reasons. If it does not do so, it is deemed to have given its consent. It may object where it believes that the employer did not take sufficient account of social aspects, or the dismissal amounts to a nonobservance of one of the guidelines referred to above, or the employee could have been kept on at another job in the same or another establishment after a reasonable amount of training/further training or after a mutually acceptable change in the individual's employment contract (§ 102 (3) WCA).

There is also what is known as a works council "right of veto" under Section 99 of the Works Constitution Act. In companies normally employing 21 or more employees with voting rights, the employer has a duty to notify the works council in advance of any recruitment, grading, regarding, and transfer of individuals, provide it with supporting documentation, and seek its consent. The works council can refuse its consent in 6 instances. One such instance is where the staff movement would constitute a breach of any act, ordinance, safety regulation, or collective agreement. Another is where the staff movement would be in default of guidelines for the selection of employees set down under § 95 (1) of the WCA. For the works council veto to be effective it must be communicated in writing to the employer within one week of being informed. Failure to comply is deemed consent. Even if the works council refuses its consent, the employer may still apply to the labor court for a decision in lieu of consent.

Finally, the works council can negotiate social compensation plans (*Sozialpläne*) and works agreements (*Betriebsvereinbarungen*). In the event of the alterations involving substantial prejudice to employees noted earlier (e.g., reduction in operations in or closure of the whole or important departments of the establishment), if consultations between the works council and the employer fail to lead to agreement on how to "reconcile their interests," either side may petition the conciliation committee to formulate a compromise plan or decision (They may earlier file for mediation under the auspices of the Federal Employment Agency.) The conciliation committee has to take into account the social interests of the employees concerned and the financial condition of the firm (§ 112 (5) WCA).

Social plans are special case of works agreements. These set down the outcome of negotiations between the works council and management—as well as awards of the conciliation committee. Although the Works Constitution Act makes explicit provision for the execution of joint decisions through such agreements, it also rules out agreements relating to wages and other conditions of employment that have been fixed or are normally fixed by collective agreement unless a collective agreement expressly authorizes the negotiation of supplementary works agreements (§ 77 (3) WCA).

As a matter of fact, framework collective agreements have increasingly made provision for their supplementation at local level. But beyond this, there is every indication that plant level agreements have ranged well beyond those prescribed by the law and, in particular, those areas where the works council has enforceable codetermination rights (Müller-Jentsch, 1995, pp. 60–61). We shall of course return to this theme of the proliferation of works agreements in examining evidence of works council rent seeking (see chapters 4 through 6), simply noting here that formal agreement is not strictly necessary for such behavior. Merely by threatening to be uncooperative in those areas where their consent is necessary, works councils can informally extend their authority to issues that are nowhere covered by the statute.

We note that the above concatenation of information, consultation, and participation rights are unique to Germany and also that they are graduated or increasing in employment size.

2.3.1.3 Incidence and Coverage of Works Councils
As we have seen, the impetus behind the 2001 Works Constitution Act was the diagnosis of the *Kommission Mitbestimmung* (1998) of a (growing) "codetermination-free zone" in which there was neither works

council presence nor (parity) board level representation. Before considering works council frequency and coverage in detail, therefore, the material in table 2.1 simply reproduces the *Kommission's* statistics on coverage for composite measure of codetermination. It can be seen that as of the mid-1990s the codetermination-free sector encompassed some 60.5 (45 percent) percent of all private sector (private and public sector) employees, both values representing material increases in the codetermination "deficit" over the situation in 1984. Again note that these calculations treat zero worker board level representation and one-third worker board level representation as equivalent (i.e., an absence of company codetermination).

Despite the lack of official data, information from several sources has in fact long confirmed that large numbers of establishments and employees in the private sector do not have works councils (see, for example, Addison, Schnabel, and Wagner, 1997; Dilger, 2002; Frick and Sadowski, 1995). In table 2.2 we provide some representative information on works council incidence and coverage by establishment size, using data from Institute for Employment Research or IAB (*Institut für Arbeitsmarkt- und Berufsforschung*) Establishment Panel. The data are for the private and public sectors combined and cover establishments with five or more employees (recall this is the minimum size of

Table 2.1 Estimates of the Fraction of Employees Covered by Codetermination at Company *and* Plant Level in 1984 and 1994/1996

Type of Codetermination	Whole Economy		Private Sector	
	1984	1994/96	1984	1994/96
Dual	22.2	18.2	30.5	24.5
Single	40.8	36.9	18.9	15.0
None	37.0	44.9	50.6	60.5

Notes: "Dual" codetermination refers to coverage through the joint presence of parity representation on supervisory boards at company level (including *Montanmitbestimmung*) and works councils at plant level. "Single" codetermination refers to coverage via works council presence at plant level but at best one-third employee representation on company boards. "None" refers to zero coverage because of the joint absence of works councils and parity representation on supervisory boards (although workers might still be covered under the 1952 Act). There are no worker directors in the public sector (included in *Whole Economy*). Data for the more recent period were compiled by the *Kommission* from a variety of sources observed in either 1994 or 1996.

Source: Kommission Mitbestimmung (1998), Tables 1 and 2, pp. 53–54.

Table 2.2 Incidence and Coverage of Works Councils in Germany in 2007 (in percent)

No. of employees	Western Germany			Eastern Germany			Germany		
	Incidence[a]	Coverage[b]	Share[c]	Incidence[a]	Coverage[b]	Share[c]	Incidence[a]	Coverage[b]	Share[c]
5–20	6.1	7.7	25.2	6.1	8.1	25.6	6.1	7.8	25.5
21–50	22.0	23.5	15.0	26.8	28.6	16.4	22.9	24.5	15.2
51–100	43.5	44.4	11.9	45.6	46.1	13.4	43.9	44.8	12.2
101–200	69.7	70.4	11.9	65.6	66.4	13.0	68.9	69.7	12.1
201–500	82.4	83.6	14.4	77.6	78.0	13.9	81.6	82.6	14.4
> 500	91.1	92.5	21.6	89.8	93.2	17.7	90.9	92.6	20.9
Average	13.0	51.2		13.8	48.9		13.2	50.8	

[a] Denotes the proportion of establishments in the class interval having works councils.
[b] Denotes the proportion of employees in the class interval employed in firms with councils.
[c] Denotes the employment share of the class interval.

Source: IAB Establishment Panel.

establishment that may elect a works council). They reveal a pattern of spotty works council incidence among smaller establishments and correspondingly low employment coverage. The proportion of workplaces with works councils is still under one-half (as is the share of employment represented by works council establishments) for plants with 51–100 employees. Works council incidence and coverage continues to increase in step with establishment size, although less so for eastern than for western Germany. (The direct association between works councils and establishment size can reasonably be linked to the potential influence of the works council.)[18] In overall terms, works councils are encountered in just 13.2 percent of all German establishments with 5 or more employees, even if the share of employment accounted for by works council establishments is sharply higher than this (50.8 percent). Corresponding values for 2000 were 16.3 and 53.0 percent, respectively, so that the decline in codetermination at workplace level is continuing (Addison, Bellmann, Schnabel, and Wagner, 2004).

Apart from the aim of increasing works council penetration among small and medium-sized enterprises, via simplified voting procedures and increased incentives for employees to get more strongly involved in the works council, it was the stated goal of the administration to increase the number of works councilors and to improve works council operation. To the latter end, the 2001 Act provides that works councils are to be provided with modern information and communication equipment and improved access to internal and external experts, as well as the opportunity to delegate tasks to working groups. In addition, as we have seen, proviso is made for more paid full-time works councilors.

Each measure to a smaller or greater degree implies an increase in the costs of operating a works council. The costs have exclusively to be borne by employers. Mid-size establishments are likely to be most affected. For example, an establishment employing 200 employees now has for the first time to bear the costs of one paid full-time works councilor. This development alone represents an increase in its wage bill of one-half of one percent.

The Federal government accepted that there were cost implications, noting in the preamble to its draft legislation of November 2000 that: "Democracy is not cost neutral. This principle also applies to democracy at the workplace and to the resulting system of establishment-level codetermination." But it proceeded to argue that: "The benefit of an operational system of codetermination outweighs the additional expense."[19] Elaboration of this argument is contained in the justification for the actual legislation: "The additional costs to the establishment have to be set against the advantages from worker participation. Codetermination establishes trust. This trust facilitates flexible and process-open forms of cooperation and thus, for example, lowers transaction costs in the establishment. In addition, employees who know that their interests are represented in the firm and works councils that are able to incorporate these interests into the decision making process can increase the productivity of the undertaking and thence the competitiveness of the German economy (see *Kommission Mitbestimmung*, 1998, p. 64, paras. 22–23)."[20]

This line of official reasoning is notable in two respects. First, the language of the *Kommission Mitbestimmung*, on which the government draws, is in practice much more guarded, stating that, at the theoretical level, it is not possible to determine a priori which of the works council's two "faces" (efficiency raising and efficiency detracting) dominates. Second, the *Kommission* interprets the empirical evidence at that time as "equivocal." (On each point, see *Kommission Mitbestimmung*, 1998, paras. 5.22, 5.14, pp. 61, 64). The bottom line is that the 2001 reform of the Works Constitution Act occasioned controversy over what had become an increasingly accepted institution.

2.3.2 More on Company Codetermination

At first blush, the sentiments of the *Kommission Mitbestimmung* (1998) on board level membership are also more guarded than those of the

Biedenkopf Commission (2006), which argued that employee representation at supervisory board level was no hindrance to a positive evaluation of Germany as a place to do business. Thus, while holding that German supervisory boards were no less competent on average than corporate governing bodies lacking codetermination, the *Kommission* acknowledged the bad press that such codetermination received aboard even if that was "mistaken" and needed to be corrected (*Kommissiom Mitbestimmung*, 1998, paras 8.23, 10.22, pp. 102, 126). For its part, Biedenkopf stated that board level representation was not a source of competitive disadvantage to Germany in terms of foreign direct investment or a "codetermination discount" in capital markets, while only a few cases of companies avoiding board level representation were known.

But such differences are clearly minor. More importantly, both reports see the goal (of modernizing codetermination) as less one of improving economic competitiveness than providing employees with a democratic voice in decisions that affect them. In the case of boardroom representation, for example, the company is seen as a social grouping in which the owners, company management, and employees work together with a common purpose. For this reason democratic participation through board level representation is still viewed as essential. The cooperative approach of the German system of employee involvement is seen as having positive impacts on the motivation and sense of responsibility of employees and important social effects through its contribution to the maintenance of social harmony. These sentiments are echoed by the *Kommission Mitbestimmung* that emphasizes throughout the importance of the creation of cooperative corporate cultures for both *betriebliche Mitbestimmung* and *Unternehmensmitbestimmung*. It was up to companies to take advantage of the productivity provided by cooperation.

2.4 Conclusions

This concludes our introduction to the two institutions of codetermination in Germany: *betriebliche Mitbestimmung* and *Unternehmensmitbestimmung*. We have traced the history of each. In the case of workplace codetermination this extends back to the heady revolutionary days of 1848 and the abortive discussions of the Constituent National Assembly in Frankfurt to set up factory committees. In the case of codetermination at enterprise level, the history is both more recent and also more fraught (e.g., the employer challenge to the constitutionality of the 1976 Codetermination Act).

It might be argued from the growing competence of the works council under law that, despite recent scandals at Volkswagen AG, plant level codetermination has come of age. That said, it is part of the dual system of industrial relations whose other element, collective bargaining, is under challenge (union density has fallen from around 51 percent in 1951 to a little over 20 percent today), and it is often argued that it will be difficult to achieve cooperative relations between works council and employers without the help of collective agreements. For its part, works council frequency and coverage is at best spotty in firms with fewer than 50 employees. To be sure, the most recent changes in the law have sought to facilitate works council formation, but there are few indications that this has succeeded. Indeed, the opposite appears to be the case (Bellmann and Ellguth, 2006). Any such tendency toward decline has repercussions in turn for collective bargaining: how, for example, can collectively agreed framework agreements and minimum standards be implemented in a differentiated way without effective plant level codetermination. On the narrower question of the decline in codetermination, the issue that arises here is whether this trend actually translates into a participation deficit. Here the roles of alternative institutional representative bodies at plant level and potentially alternative direct participative mechanisms are only now beginning to receive attention. In the latter context, for example, Addison, Schnabel, and Wagner (2000b, 2000c) reported at the time that a very substantial proportion of small and medium-sized companies *without* works councils embraced teamworking and also engaged in active discussion with affected employees about of planned investments in machinery. Such forms of direct participation may prove more effective than indirect participation via the works council alone. In short, codetermination-free should not, it seems, be equated with an absence of participation.

Company codetermination is more clearly at the crossroads. There is widespread opposition of employers to any one-size-fits-all revision of the 1976 Act and considerable debate as to the economic consequences of worker directors. As we have implied, there is scant indication of German company codetermination having been adopted by the wider market. Indeed, regime competition between forms of incorporation might intensify in the future. These issues will be taken up in subsequent chapters, even if some other pressing topics such as the scope for *financial participation*, long neglected in Germany, will not.

Finally, both the Biedenkopf Commission and the earlier *Kommission Mitbestimmung* have taken the view that economic analysis does not inform policy because the theory and the econometric evidence is equivocal *and* because efficiency considerations are of decidedly secondary importance. We will examine both assertions. The notion that social harmony and social cohesion are pro-productive inputs also requires scrutiny. In offering an economic interpretation we hope to provide a more balanced view as to whether or not codetermination is a hindrance to *Standort Deutschland*.

CHAPTER 3

The Theory of Codetermination

3.1 Introduction

In this chapter we investigate the theory of *Mitbestimmung*. Much of our discussion will pertain to works councils or *betriebliche Mitbestimmung*, although on a number of occasions we will touch on themes subsequently encountered in our treatment of worker representation on company boards or *Unternehmensmitbestimmung* (see chapter 7). The case for works councils rests on much the same arguments as have been used to justify unions in Anglo-Saxon countries. Among other things, these include issues of governance (or contract enforcement) in circumstances where labor market contracts are incomplete (and ignore many contingencies) and, more encompassing, on notions of "collective voice." The collective voice model was offered to balance if not counter the view of *unions* as combinations in restraint of trade, namely, as labor monopolies that adversely impact efficiency by distorting factor prices and usage, redirecting higher quality workers (and capital) from higher to lower marginal product uses, and also by engaging the polity. Interestingly, however, it soon became clear that the *works council* rather than the union might be the exemplar of collective voice. It was therefore no accident that one of the architects of collective voice proposed the first purpose-built model of the works council. In what follows, we offer a critical examination of these arguments while also addressing possible alternatives to works councils.

3.2 Incomplete Contracting

In real world labor markets characterized by long-term relations, contracts are often incomplete and open ended because of the difficulty of writing complete contingent claims contracts that anticipate all future circumstances and set down in precise terms how the parties will react to each and every new development. Because of transaction costs, therefore, the contracts that instead result are incomplete or implicit. In such circumstances some mechanism has thus to be found to ensure that the parties to the contract are motivated to follow its terms, without recourse to constant bargaining/renegotiation with all the ensuing possibilities for opportunistic behavior that could dissipate the joint surplus.

There is now an extensive contract-theoretic literature covering such continuity labor markets (see, for example, the contributions in Rosen, 1994). Extending beyond its initial focus on differential risk aversion, the literature illustrates how implicit contracts can cope with asymmetric information to make truth revelation the appropriate strategy (by restricting the choices open to the firm), while dealing with the enforcement problem (by penalizing firms that renege on future contract delivery through a reputation effects mechanism that means they then have to pay a permanently higher wage for their transgressions).

More concretely perhaps, in the idiosyncratic or nonstandard exchange version of contract theory (see Williamson, Wachter, and Harris, 1975) there emerges a distinct governance apparatus geared to maximizing the joint surplus of the firm by suppressing the hazards of unconstrained idiosyncratic trading. The key elements of this apparatus are the use of promotion ladders, formal grievance procedures, and the application of the seniority principle; all of which elements are components of a structured internal labor market whose central function is to police and enforce incomplete contracts.

As initially developed, there is no mention of worker representative agencies in contract theory. Contracts are either automatically self-enforcing or there is a nonunion governance apparatus with procedural safeguards. The characterization of the union as a commitment device was first advanced by Malcomson (1983) in discussing a situation in which uncertainty in the form of product market demand shocks encourages the use of *contingent* contracts to allocate risk between risk-averse employers and workers. However, such contracts are unenforceable because neither the courts nor the workers can observe the state of the world. But unions can provide workers with more accurate information about the state of nature. Coordinated action via the union thus permits workers to enforce an efficient, state contingent contract.[1]

But in practice the union role has most commonly been invoked in the context of employer opportunism arising in the case of worker investments in firm-specific training. Where workers make such reliance investments, postcontractually the employer might exploit the workers' dependency upon the firm—recall that unlike general training, these investments only have value in the firm—and appropriate their share of the quasi-rents resulting from these investments. This is known as the "hold-up" problem, with firms holding up the sunk investments of workers in their training The outcome is an underinvestment in specific human capital by the worker.

The idea is that the union, or some other worker representation agency such as a works council, could act to prevent the hold-up problem by making the firm honor its commitments (Menezes-Filho and Van Reenen, 2003). As a result, the amount of specific training undertaken can move closer to the optimum.[2]

Latterly, the argument has been generalized to encompass effort input by Hogan (2001), who argues that by monitoring the employment relation between the firm and its workers the union provides the latter with valuable information (since effort expenditure is costly) on whether the firm is honoring its commitments under implicit contracts. There cannot be recourse to the courts because although effort is observed by both sides it is not verifiable. In these circumstances, the union becomes the substitute extra-legal agency, disciplining the firm for a breach of the implicit contract. In turn, the union gives credibility to the employer's promises of ex post compensation, ex ante compensation being ruled out on moral hazard grounds. As a result, employment levels are cet. par. higher under unionism.

This is of course but one side of the rent-seeking coin and we will have occasion in this and succeeding chapters to visit union hold-up of *firm* quasi-rents stemming from long-lived investments in physical and intangible capital. But we might mention here that union decline in Hogan's application of the implicit contract model is explained not by employer opposition but by more comprehensive legal coverage of the employment relation. To quote Hogan (2001, p. 192), "The decreased demand for union services may actually be seen as a victory for workers who no longer need to rely on implicit contracting to secure essential benefits in the workplace."

Summarizing, a prima facie case can be made that worker representation agencies can facilitate efficient contracting in situations where there is a long-term relation between the two sides but where employers' ex ante promises to take workers' interests into account are not credible or where the reputation effects mechanism is weak.

3.3 Collective Voice

The collective voice model builds on Hirschmann's (1970) exit-voice (and loyalty) paradigm. It is a model of the organized labor market wherein worker quits substitute for customer switching (or exit) and union voice substitutes for customer complaints about the product (or customer voice). Faced with a divergence between desires and actual conditions at the workplace, the worker can quit and search for better employment. Alternatively, via the agency of the union, the worker can instead engage in voice, discussing with the employer the conditions that need changing.[3]

As developed by Freeman (1976, 1978, 1980) and Freeman and Medoff (1979, 1983, 1984), collective voice has a number of distinct components. Before addressing these, however, we must also recognize the overall setting in which it is located. First of all, the model recognizes that unions have a monopoly side as well. These two faces of unionism—rent-seeking behavior and the expression of collective voice—coexist. Second, the model is more properly described as a *collective voice-institutional response* model. That is to say, much hinges on management's response. The potential gains pointed to by the model can be thwarted by an unfavorable response on the part of management to collective bargaining—or by an adverse reaction by the union to any reorganization of the work process. In other words, voice cannot succeed without appropriate institutional responses.[4] In the light of these arguments, it can be seen that net impact of the union/voice entity on performance is an empirical question par excellence.

Of the various aspects of collective voice the best known is the union role in providing information. The labor market context is important here: it is (largely) one of continuity rather than spot market contracting because of on-the-job skills specific to the firm and the costs attaching to worker mobility and turnover. Given the informational problem in continuity markets, what mechanisms are available to elicit information on worker preferences and sources of discontent? Quit behavior can provide such information either inferentially or directly (via exit interviews) but such information may suffer from selection biases, from problems of motivating the worker to disclose information when there is no obvious benefit to him or her from doing so, and finally from the sheer cost of the process of trial and error in discovering the efficacy of contractual innovations.

Collective voice, via the agency of a union—or analogous workplace organization—may outperform individual voice for a variety of reasons.

One is the public goods aspect of the workplace. Nonrival consumption of shared working conditions and common workplace rules create a public goods problem of preference revelation. Without some collective form of organization, there will be too little incentive for the individual to reveal his or her preferences since action of the part of others may produce the public good at no cost to that individual. Unions collect information on the preferences of all workers and *aggregate* them to determine the social demand for such goods. Substituting average preferences for marginal preferences and arbitraging them may be efficient, assuming the union is a pure agent of the member principal and that autonomous representative bodies are the only form of collective voice.

A further public goods dimension of the workplace stems from the nature of the effort input. Without some form of collective organization, and assuming there are significant complementarities in worker effort inputs, the incentive of the individual to take into account the effects of his or her actions on others may be too small, just as with preference revelation. In other words, collective organization may potentially increase output through a joint determination of effort inputs.[5] In some sense, the union may be construed as the agent of the employer principal in monitoring worker effort (Bryson, 2004a).

The expression of collective voice is thus expected to reduce quits and absenteeism. And the reduction in quits is expected to lower hiring and training costs and increase investments in firm-specific human capital. Lower quits may also occasion less disruption in the functioning of work groups.

This, then, is the information aspect of collective voice.[6] The remaining aspects of collective voice are *influence* and *governance*. The issue of influence is related to the conventional "shock effect" of unionism, whereby having to pay a union premium forces management into looking for cost savings elsewhere (e.g., Freeman and Medoff, 1984, p. 15). But it is secondary to the issue of governance, to which aspect we next turn.

Governance refers to the policing or monitoring of incomplete employment contracts, encountered earlier. Freeman (1976, p. 364) and Freeman and Medoff (1984, p. 11) argue that the union governance apparatus of the collective voice model is quite consistent with the modern contracts literature. They contend that the presence of a union can make it easier to engage in long-term efficient contracting of this nature. Thus, the presence of a union specializing in information about the contract and in the representation of workers can prevent employers from engaging in opportunistic behavior. Workers may withhold effort and cooperation when the employer cannot credibly commit to take their interests into account. Thus, fearing dismissal, workers may be unwilling to invest in firm-specific skills or disclose information facilitating pro-productive innovations at the workplace. The formation of a union and the introduction of a system of industrial jurisprudence is one way of protecting the employees. In this way, unions may generate worker cooperation, including the introduction of efficiency-enhancing work practices.

The threat of credible punishment implies bargaining power. And bargaining power in turn implies rent seeking. As we have seen, in acknowledging the monopoly face of unions, Freeman and Medoff do not deny that rent seeking occurs—even if they do rather overaccentuate the positive. Having identified the union Janus, as it were, they then embark on a comprehensive empirical analysis of union effects. In the process, they spawned a new literature.

In his wide-ranging review of that literature, Hirsch (2004) interprets the developing U.S. evidence on unions and economic performance as less favorable to unions than Freeman and Medoff contend, subject to some inevitable disputation over causality. First, the average union productivity effect is close to zero. Second, there is an absence of large positive productivity growth effects. Third, unions reduce profitability.[7] The latter result is conceded by Freeman and Medoff, although they argue that it is essentially redistributive (i.e., the result of a capture of monopoly rents). Hirsch argues to the contrary that monopoly profits associated with industry concentration are not a source of union gains. Fourth, and relatedly, U.S. unions appropriate the returns from investments in tangible and intangible capital. That is to say, there is a *union* hold-up problem: union rent seeking captures some of the share of quasi-rents that make up the normal returns to investments in long-lived capital and R&D. There is also an indirect union tax on investment via reduced profitability that is roughly of the same magnitude as the direct effect in reducing investment in physical capital but less than this in the case of R&D. Both the direct and indirect taxes serve to reduce investment (see also Hirsch, 1991).

We cite these results to indicate that union rent seeking might undermine the union voice solution to the information and governance problems of continuity markets. Having said that, the next theoretical development to which now turn recognizes the problem and seeks to attenuate rent seeking through institutional innovation while retaining the advantages of collective voice. The U.S. literature remains a useful benchmark for ascertaining the extent to which this perceived attenuation has proven successful and its themes a useful organizing device in discussing the empirical literature of chapters 4 through 6.

3.4   Enter the Works Council

Subsequent development of the union voice model recognizes the bargaining problem up front. In Freeman and Lazear's (1995) purpose-built analysis of the works council it is accepted that works councils will always demand too much authority or competence so that limits have to be placed on their bargaining power and hence potential rent seeking ability. And for these authors the wider German institutional infrastructure fits the bill in this regard.

Freeman and Lazear argue that the machinery of the works council holds out the prospect of an improvement in the joint surplus of the enterprise because of information exchange, consultation, and participation (i.e., codetermination). Let us consider each element of this worker involvement continuum in turn. Beginning with information, and following Freeman and Lazear, let us assume that the firm and its workers decide on just one workplace variable, namely, the speed of work. (We have earlier argued more widely that, by collecting information about the preferences of all workers, agencies such as the works council can enable the firm to choose a more efficient mix of personnel policies, as well as providing an alternative to exit.) There are two speeds, fast and normal, and two states of nature, good and bad. Profits are positive irrespective of how fast workers work in the good state. They are also positive when workers work at a fast pace in the adverse state, but they are negative if they work at a slow pace. Management's use of the works council as a communicator to workers about the state of nature can lead them to work harder in the bad state of nature since in the absence of credible information—equated by the authors with a legal requirement to disclose financial information—workers might be tempted to discount management claims as to the seriousness of the situation. These claims might simply be viewed as opportunistic or strategic, leading workers instead to reduce the pace of work and the firm to make a loss and ultimately go out of business. Having access to information that can verify management's claims, the works council can render them credible and promote increased effort when it is needed to sustain then viability of the firm.[8]

Next, consultation for its part allows new solutions to production and other workplace problems by virtue of the nonoverlapping information sets of the two sides *and* the creativity of discussion (i.e., labor and management combine information and effort and hence "new ideas are spawned" [Freeman and Lazear, 1995, p. 44]. The authors caution, however, that the effectiveness of consultation depends on the amount of delay occasioned by the process.

The final element is participation or codetermination. Such rights are said to generate an improvement in the joint surplus by providing workers with greater security that encourages them to take a longer-run view of the prospects of the firm. (However, the median voter model might produce the opposite result by virtue of the preponderance of older employees in worker representative agencies.) Familiarly, workers will then invest more in firm-specific training and offer workplace concessions that will improve the productivity of capital.

These are the advantages of increased employee involvement. The downside is the attendant growth in worker bargaining power. The joint surplus will not continue to grow with the authority of the works council institution. This is more than just an issue of reduced managerial prerogative because it is argued that the worker share in the joint surplus grows with the surplus while profit falls both relatively and absolutely. The workers' share rises because knowledge and involvement are power. The same factors that cause the surplus to grow will also cause profit to fall. Workers are depicted as demanding too much involvement precisely because their share will continue to rise after the joint surplus has peaked. Equivalently, employers will either resist work councils or vest them with insufficient power. To quote Freeman and Lazear (1995, p. 29), "If councils increase the rent going to workers more than they increase total rent, firms will oppose them. It is better to have a quarter slice of a 12-inch pie than an eighth slice of a 16-inch pie."

Since the social-welfare-maximizing power of the works council exceeds the level that management would freely choose to cede it, the presumption is that the works council will have to be mandated. But since the optimum competence of the works council lies between what management would voluntarily offer and the amount workers will demand some limits have to be placed on the works council. It is at this point that the wider institutional structure intervenes.

The German situation commends itself to Freeman and Lazear because of the practical limits placed on rent seeking. Narrowing these down, we have seen that councils are excluded from reaching agreement with the employer on wages and working conditions that are settled or normally settled by collective agreement between unions and employers at industry or regional level, without express authorization to the contrary. Further, the German enabling legislation forbids works councils from going on strike under the "peace obligation" of the Works Constitution Act. Historically, works councils have been enjoined to work together with the employer in a spirit of mutual trust for the good of the employees and the establishment. As a result, it is conjectured that a German-like system may allow a decoupling of the factors that determine the size of the joint surplus from factors that determine its distribution.[9]

The strength of the Freeman and Lazear model is that it recognizes rent seeking by workers through the agency of the works council. The authors show why it is logical for employers to resist works councils (or strong works councils) and their argument for a mandate is more compelling than in prisoner's dilemma models based on precontractual asymmetric information (see chapter 7). Freeman and Lazear are prepared to countenance a reduction in the firm surplus as long as the joint surplus is increased by a mandate. But note the imprecision of the model at this point. The authors leave open the question of whether the institutional constraints they favor are sufficient. The key element in the model, then, is the *potential* decoupling of the factors that determine the size of the surplus from those that determine its division or distribution. Once again, the efficiency of the institution is ultimately an empirical question. Our next three chapters will be given over to the growing empirical analysis devoted to this question. Before then, however, we need to ask whether there are realistic alternatives to the works council, a question that also arises in the case of unions.

3.5   Alternative Institutions?

A final consideration is, then, whether there exist alternative institutions to works councils. Our opening statement is of course that much of the force of the argument favoring (influential) works councils hinges on continuity markets. Where there is not a long-term relation between the two sides, where reliance investments are not being made, much of the case evaporates. Also, in small firms with an owner-manager not only are agency problems sidestepped but the informational problem is also much attenuated.

Further, as we have noted, continuity markets should not be uncritically linked with works councils. To repeat, and as Jirjahn and Smith (2006, p. 656) note, "if the employer is interested in a long-term, high-trust relationship with the workforce, and employees have enough information about the economic situation of the firm, the repeated games mechanism may work even without the presence of a works council to enforce it."

Abstracting here from the existence of very similar but *nonautonomous* institutions, namely, other "company-specific forms of employee representation" (such as the presence of am employee spokesperson or round table conferences, and so on),[10] what specific potential substitutes are available? What we have in mind is employee involvement/ high performance work practices (EI/HPWPs). Although there is no settled definition, the term typically includes profit sharing schemes, share ownership arrangements, consultative bodies, teamworking, quality circles and problem solving groups, briefing groups, systematic use of the management chain to communicate, regular meetings with senior management, benchmarking, total quality management, training, job security, job rotation, and payment for skill acquisition (see, inter alia, Ichniowski, 1990; Ichniowski and Shaw, 1995; Huselid, 1995; Wood and de Menezes, 1998; Cappelli and Neumark, 2001). As will become clear, many of the same arguments used in the collective voice model again come into play.

The starting point in the EI/HPWP model is the notion that workplace innovations change the production function in such a way as to increase the productivity of labor and other inputs. The basic premise is by now familiar: workers have important private information and valuable insights into how to improve their jobs. There is scope for beneficial trades once workers are trained and presented with opportunities to exercise their skills through job redesign, decreased supervision, and involvement in decision making, and are motivated to contribute through productivity bonuses.

EI/HPWPs work by encouraging workers to work harder (e.g., as a result of job enrichment) and smarter (reflecting the input of the worker in efficient job design), and by inducing structural changes that improve performance. The latter include cross-training and flexible job assignment, which can reduce the cost of absenteeism; decentralized decision making to self-managed teams, permitting a reduction in line management while benefiting communication; and training in problem solving and computer skills, which can increase the benefits of new technologies. Innovative practices thus lead to other pro-productive changes.

It is conventional to argue that the various strands of employee involvement are interdependent and mutually reinforcing: the complementarities thesis. This is the notion of "bundling," namely, the idea that such innovative practices are more effective when combined with supporting management practices (Milgrom and Roberts, 1995). As an example of one such cluster, compensation schemes like profit sharing can incentivize employee involvement, while information disclosure and training can improve worker decisions at the same time as job security encourages them to take a long-run view of the firm and make suggestions. Another example might be the potential synergies between job rotation, self-managed teams, and payment for skill acquisition.

The role of profit sharing (and share ownership) is of particular interest because it is thought to increase productivity by linking one part of pay to firm performance, thereby aligning worker interests with those of the undertaking. The effects are both direct and indirect. The direct effects cover the immediate effort incentives, although these are reduced in proportion to the number of employees sharing the benefits.[11] The indirect effect comes about by educating workers about the link between pay and performance, reassuring them that increased productivity will not result in layoffs/redundancies, and increasing identification with the firm or improving worker morale or job satisfaction. Worker sorting effects may add to efficiency where profit sharing attracts more able while reducing the risk that the most able will quit, and accelerating the departure of the least able (Bryson and Freeman, 2007, p. 8).

In turn, the link with employee decision-making autonomy is potentially crucial. Workers are likely to be offered substantial decision-making autonomy where they have better knowledge about the work process than the supervisor or manager. Again, these are exactly the circumstances in which we would expect the employer to use profit sharing or other financial reward systems to incentivize workers to make the right decisions as well share their valuable private information. (There is also the practical point that workers who are asked to exercise higher responsibility will become demotivated unless compensated.) It is likely therefore that there will be a link between profit sharing and analogous group-based performance pay systems.[12]

Since many of the above arguments are consonant with the collective voice model, the obvious issue that now arises is whether some traditional or autonomous form of employee representation (like a union or a works council) is required. Opinion is divided. Some would see little difference in the arguments for workplace representation and EI/HPWPs.[13] This is most obviously the case, however, where there is some means of decoupling production from distribution issues.

The two remaining positions are that the institutions are either substitutes or Edgeworth complements. Thus, the decline of worker representation in many countries, taken in association with the growth in EI/HPWPs, may be taken as an indication that the two are substitutes by design or effect (where, by enhancing worker satisfaction, they reduce the demand for worker representation). Alternatively, observers have often contended that traditional workplace representation through unions or works councils is important to the success of innovative work practices for several reasons. First, they provide the assurance that a serious hearing will be given to employees' suggestions. Second, they have access to higher levels of management. Third, they create a better participatory environment by providing contractual protection against arbitrary management actions, or because of a more sustained commitment to EI/HPWPs in such regimes made possible by their longer-term employment relations and narrower pay and status differentials (Cooke, 1994, pp. 597–598). Finally, albeit backhandedly, EI/HPWPs might offer a bigger payoff in union regimes with the elimination of restrictive/protective work practices.

3.6 Conclusions

Our review of the theoretical issues began with the notion that competitive labor markets often diverge from simple spot markets. The employment relation can instead be long lived with workers enjoying near-lifetime employment and making a series of reliance investments in their firms. An entire literature has grown up around the necessarily incomplete contracts that emerge in such markets and how they can be automatically self-enforcing without the hazard of exploitation by *either* side.

But equally there has been a sharp debate on whether such contracts stand alone or whether collective representation through unions might not help in their execution and performance. Unions can help verify employer statements as to the state of nature and at the same time make employer promises more credible. This debate continued independently of the next important development charted in this chapter, namely, the notion of collective voice. In addition to governance issues, this new view of unions emphasized the public goods nature of the workplace and how the substitution of an average for a marginal calculus could result in a profound improvement in the terms and conditions of employment.

The difficulties with the collective voice are twofold. First and most importantly, there is the issue of rent seeking. Second, the precise mechanisms through which unions can improve matters are disturbingly vague apart from the beneficial consequences of reduced labor turnover. Leaving aside the latter for the moment, the rent seeking problem may dominate—at least in Anglo-Saxon regimes. In particular, the U.S. literature at least has suggested that the capture of firm profits is not efficiency neutral because of the implications for investment (part of the profits are normal returns to long-lived investments). Whether company unions might avoid these problems is an unknown because they are precluded under Section 8(a)2 of the 1935 National Labor Relations Act.

There followed a reworking of the collective voice model to address the rent seeking problem. The influential works council model of Freeman and Lazear (1995) is compelling in that it makes understandable the opposition of employers to systems of worker representation that are capable of increasing the joint surplus of the enterprise as well underscoring the concerns of public policy that arise from workers demanding too much influence, and increases in their surplus that ultimately lead to a decline of the joint surplus. The authors' purpose-built model of the works council emphasized the importance of limits on the competence of that institution. The suggestion is that the German institutional setting provides for a decoupling of production from and distribution issues because of the particular attribution of bargaining authority under the dual system in which the works council is embedded *and* the peace obligation imposed on works councils by successive Works Constitution Acts. *Vulgo*: German works councils offer scope for material productivity gains without the downside risk.

Nevertheless there are no guarantees. The theory offers no blueprint describing the optimal legal boundaries of works council authority. And works councils might still be too powerful de facto. In the final part of the chapter, therefore, we looked to potential alternatives to works councils that might further narrow the downside risk as it were. We identified a number of employee involvement/high performance work practices that have actually grown in importance as both unionism and codetermination have declined. We identified potential clusters of such practices, most important perhaps those combining employee decision-making autonomy with financial participation. But the association between declining codetermination and the growth in such practices in no way establishes causality. It may yet be that innovative works practices are complementary with works council. This discussion therefore raised a number of fresh empirical lines of inquiry while flagging the autonomy issue.

Finally, we should mention a lacuna of the theories reviewed here. This concerns the representativeness of unions and works councils as well as agency considerations on the other side of the market.[14] We have considered some aspects of agency here, as when unions might monitor effort input on the part of workers or where profit sharing might help align the interests of workers and shareholders. But relaxation of the assumption that worker representative bodies, unions or works councils, and management are pure agents of their respective principals might have interesting implications for performance. In chapter 7 we will review one interesting such application that links works councils to self-enforcing contracts and agency with trust in organizations.[15] One of its results is that works councils may have a bigger effect on performance when no profit sharing for managers is in place. This could be because profit sharing decreases the commitment value of agency and workers councils cannot function effectively without management cooperation. Public choice theoretic considerations deserve more attention than they have been accorded in the literature, not least because they may assist in helping identify differences in types of works council and works council impact.

CHAPTER 4

The Early Econometric Literature on Works Councils

4.1 Introduction

In this chapter we review initial attempts to quantify the effect of works councils on firm performance along the dimensions of profitability, total factor productivity, value-added, investment, innovation, and labor turnover. The studies we review cover a rich range of performance outcomes. One limitation is that they are all are based on small samples of establishments of firms. Thus, we will have to see how well the results stack up against findings from larger samples. Accordingly, in chapter 5 we will consider studies exploring the Hanover Firm Panel and the NIFA Panel, covering manufacturing industry in Lower Saxony and the national machine tool industry, respectively. And in chapter 6 we will turn to results from a truly nationally representative data set, namely, the Establishment Panel of the Institute for Employment Research of the Federal Employment Agency (*Institut für Arbeitsmarkt- und Berufsforschung der Bundesagentur für Arbeit*), or *IAB-Betriebspanel*.

To anticipate some of what follows, and following Addison, Schnabel, and Wagner (2004), we will argue that German research conforms to three main phases of activity. Curiously enough the literature follows a reverse path—for some considerable time at least—to that taken by the corresponding U.S. *union* literature, where the initial result that unions increase total factor productivity by upwards of 20 percent (Brown and Medoff, 1978) was steadily to hemorrhage through time. More important, however, is the fact that the econometric literature has truly "grown" and convincingly moved beyond its depiction by Frege (2002, p. 239) as at a "dead end." One important aim of this and the next two chapters is to convey this point without seeking to overstate the degree of consensus reached as to the economic consequences of the works council.

4.2 Managerial Pressure/Managerial Competence Model

Perhaps the *leitmotif* of the first phase literature is the idea that poor managers get the workplace industrial relations they deserve while the most competent managers can establish effective communications without the paraphernalia of the works council. The model was first advanced by FitzRoy and Kraft (1985, 1987a, 1987b, 1990) in a series of influential papers in the decade of the 1980s that were to shape much of the then contemporary debate on codetermination. However, as we shall see, these authors' views of the institution were to change in the mid-1990s and have further evolved during the present decade (see chapter 7).

In their managerial pressure/managerial competence model FitzRoy and Kraft see works councils as external constraints on internal organization that are likely to prove particularly damaging to the efficiency of the most able managers. The latter have every incentive to provide wages and working conditions that can eliminate the need for workers to elect a council. By contrast, managers who are unable or unwilling to communicate effectively with their employees are forced into a dialogue or consultation (which could nonetheless prove beneficial to the bottom line if not the managers' peace of mind—or utility, to put it more formally). Autocratic managers may be prepared to pay the price of a bad reputation and higher turnover to indulge their tastes for the arbitrary exercise of authority. It follows that the external constraints that hamper efficient managers may have the opposite result for the autocratic or downright incompetent managers and, to the extent that they help improve communication and retention, boost productivity.

In addition to incompetent and competent managers there is said to be considerable variation in productivity and working conditions, including the pressure applied by management on workers and the levels of effort required of them. This is where the *managerial pressure* component of the model comes into play. Managers who push their workers hard to maintain above-average productivity levels will stimulate works council formation (as well as union organization more generally).

So there are some distinct lines of causation predicted by the model. Thus, works councils can lead to improvements in efficiency in inefficient settings but the absence of works councils in truly efficient organizations is hypothesized to lead to a negative association between works council presence and productivity in cross section, which is the managerial competence case. Outside these extremes of competence and incompetence, higher-than-average productivity could increase the likelihood of a works council election (the managerial pressure argument). In a simultaneous equations framework, therefore, productivity (purged of the negative effect on it of works councils) should increase the likelihood of works council formation.

Now it will be recalled that at this time the collective voice model was much in vogue. FitzRoy and Kraft's subtle model is an alternative vision that says that there is no reason why the best managers should not be able to install adequate systems of communication. Indeed, the model offers a reverse vision: "a genuine efficient voice effect of unions is thus really only plausible in initially badly managed firms" (FitzRoy and Kraft, 1985, p. 538). The break with collective voice becomes even clearer in the work of Kraft (1986) who reverts backs to the efficiency of the traditional marginal calculus in emphasizing the role of "individual" voice in ameliorating quits. Finally, the authors point to an issue of reverse causation that can potentially undermine the direction of causation from unions to improved productivity in the collective voice model. That being said, FitzRoy and Kraft have latterly come to see works councils in more positive light on contract-theoretic grounds.

4.3 Empirical Findings

Results of this first phase literature are summarized in table 4.1.[1] The hallmark of these studies is an often unfavorable association between works council presence and the particular economic outcome investigated. This is most obviously the case in the key studies by FitzRoy and Kraft (rows 1 through 3), which are also notable for their technical sophistication (in particular, use of systems of equations).

In the first three rows in the table, FitzRoy and Kraft exploit a common data set to investigate three outcome indicators: profitability (row 1), total factor productivity (row 2), and innovation (row 3). (In row 8 in the table, the authors revisit this data set to reexamine works council effects on productivity as measured by value-added—and report rather different findings.) A few words on this common data set are therefore in order. First, the data were collected in personal interviews with (West) German firms all of which were in the metal industry, approximately two-thirds from the mechanical engineering sector. Second, approximately 200 companies were randomly approached

Table 4.1 The Economic Impact of the Works Council—Phase 1 Studies

Study	Data	Dependent Variable(s)	Methodology	Findings
1. FitzRoy and Kraft (1985)	Pooled data for 1977 and 1979 on 61/62 firms in the metal-working industry.	Profitability (ratio of cash flow to capital), union density, wages, and salaries.	Four-equation system estimated by 3SLS. Detailed firm controls. Work council presence not endogenised.	Union density has a positive and statistically significant effect on profitability (and on wages and salaries). Coefficient estimate for the works council dummy is negative and statistically significant in the profit equation. But the works council effect is not statistically significant in the wage equation.
2. FitzRoy and Kraft (1987b)	As above.	Total factor productivity and works council presence.	Simultaneous weighted least squares—Probit estimates.	Work council presence associated with a significant reduction in productivity. Union density effects positive and statistically significant throughout.
3. FitzRoy and Kraft (1990)	57 metal-working firms, 1979.	Innovation, as proxied by the proportion of sales consisting of new products introduced in the preceding five years, and an "organized labor" measure derived from the interaction of the works council dummy and union density.	Simultaneous weighted least squares—Tobit estimates.	Organized labor covariate is associated with a statistically significant reduction in innovative activity.
4. Schnabel and Wagner (1994)	31 manufacturing establishments in two German states, 1990.	Proportion of revenues spent on R&D in 1979.	Single-equation Tobit model. Parsimonious specification.	Coefficient estimate for works council dummy is positive and marginally statistically significant. Union density has strongly negative effect on R&D intensity.
5. Addison, Kraft, and Wagner (1993)	c. 50– establishment sample from same data as the study in row 4, above.	Profitability, value-added, and investment.	Single-equation specifications estimated by least median of squares and reweighted least squares.	Mixed pattern of generally statistically insignificant coefficient estimates for the works council dummy variable. But the works council coefficient is negative and statistically significant in the case of investments in physical capital.

6. Addison and Wagner (1997)	74 manufacturing establishments in Lower Saxony, 1993.	Subjective measure of "high profitability" and an innovation measure (introduction of a new product in 1992).	Probit models. Three works council indicators: works council presence, degree of participation or "voice" of the works council, and an instrument for the presence of a works council.	Mixed pattern of generally statistically insignificant coefficient estimates for all three works council variables. The exception is the degree of works council involvement measure that is negatively associated with high profitability, albeit only at the 0.10 level.
7. Kraft (1986)	As for the studies in rows 1 and 2.	Subjective measure of "high quits" among unskilled workforce and a synthetic index measure of "individual voice" in for blue-collar workerseach case for unskilled workers.	Single-equation probit model of high quit rates and simultaneous equation Probit model of high quit rates and individual voice.	Individual voice, but not collective voice (as proxied by works council presence), serves to significantly reduce high turnover in each set of estimates. No evidence of a feedback effect from quits to voice.
8. FitzRoy and Kraft (1995)[a]	As for the studies in rows 1 and 2.	Productivity (value-added) and profit sharing.	Two-stage endogenous switching model seeking to control for the effect of selection of firms into profit sharing. Log-linear productivity equations for profit sharing and nonprofit sharing firms with selection arguments in each.	Works council presence associated with a statistically significant increase (decrease) in productivity in firms with (without) profit sharing. Selection coefficient is statistically insignificant in profit sharing firms. It is statistically significant and in firms without profit sharing.

[a] See also FitzRoy and Kraft (1987a).

initially, of which one-half agreed to an interview. Some 13 firms failed to provide financial data (note these are all unquoted firms) and other missing data explain the further erosion in the sample, which was basically designed to consist equally of firms with and without profit sharing. Third, the number of employees averaged 626 (with a standard deviation of 1,020). Fourth, neither the works council nor union status of the firms changed over the two years. Finally, some firms provided data for one year only.

The unifying theme of all three studies is the *managerial pressure/ managerial competence* model described earlier. Hard-driving managers are said to elicit greater effort from their workers and are rewarded with higher salaries and profits. The workers respond by joining unions, and unionized workers earn higher wages (although the authors note that this premium is only partial compensation for their greater effort). As noted earlier, workers are also more likely to form a works council on defensive grounds. But efficient managers will be able to sidestep autonomous works councils by paying higher wages.

In putting their model through its paces, FitzRoy and Kraft model the existence of worker representation; respectively, union density, works council presence, and a conflation of both measures. Thus, the profitability study by FitzRoy and Kraft (1985) in row 1 of the table examines the arrow of causation running from performance to workplace union density, as workers are supposed to react defensively to the higher demands made on them by managers. In their productivity study in row 2 of the table, the probability of the existence of a works council is simultaneously estimated with total factor productivity. FitzRoy and Kraft (1987a, p. 495) anticipate that the direction of causation will flow in two directions: first, from higher performance to workplace representation as was earlier reported for unionization and for the same (defensive) reason; and, second, from works council presence to reduced output as works councils are thought to be an "external constraint on internal organization" reducing the efficiency of the best managers who have every incentive (and the knack) to avoid them. Finally, in their innovation study in row 3 of the table, FitzRoy and Kraft (1990) consider whether unionization might have an adverse effect on productivity when taken conjunction with works councils, stiffening the resolve of the latter in conflict situations. Accordingly the authors construct a composite *organized labor* variable, combining union density and works council presence. Now the influence of union density is taken to be direct rather than indirect (as in the row 1 study).[2] The new composite workplace representation variable is jointly estimated with the level of innovative activity.

The results of this laudable attempt to endogenize workplace representation are as follows. First, in the case of financial performance, works councils appear to be associated with sharply reduced profitability (row 1). But recall that in this case it is union density that is endogenized, not works council presence. However, in their productivity analysis (row 2), works council presence is associated with lower total factor productivity. In other words, net of any positive feedback effect from productivity to works council presence, works councils appear to lead to reduced productivity. In addition, estimated productivity has a narrowly statistically significant effect on works council probability, so that support is adduced for both the managerial pressure and managerial competence hypotheses. The negative association between works council presence and productivity is the stronger result of the two relationships and is robust throughout. Unqualified productivity benefits from the formal expression of collective voice are contraindicated.

And what finally of situations in which unionism operates in tandem with works councils? Here FitzRoy and Kraft's simultaneous equation estimates of innovation—as measured by the proportion of sales consisting of new products introduced over a five-year interval—and the composite organized labor variable point to a strongly negative effect running from organization to innovation. There is no indication of reverse causality.

FitzRoy and Kraft see bureaucratization rather than rent seeking as the culprit in this unflattering portrayal of the consequences of workplace representation. Thus, in explaining their innovation findings, the authors' argue that "Union bargaining in a low trust environment is simply inimical to the flexibility which is essential for innovation and modern technology" (FitzRoy and Kraft, 1990, p. 97). Distributional factors are not held responsible for the profitability results either. Rather, these are seen as indicative of the historical preponderance of unions in currently declining industries. Taken in conjunction with their result that works councils do not raise wages,[3] FitzRoy and Kraft's findings differ sharply from the rent-seeking paradigm that dominates the U.S. union literature discussed in chapter 3. To this extent, it is perhaps less surprising to observe a sudden change in emphasis in these authors' latest reworking of data from the metal working sample. But it is appropriate that we remit our review of this study to the last row entry in table 4.1.

With the major exception of the study by Kraft (1986) in row 7 of the table, most of the remaining studies of Phase I provide single-equation estimates. They present a less unified picture of works council impact than do the (initial) analyses of FitzRoy and Kraft. That said, just one study reports evidence favorable to the works council entity, namely Schnabel and Wagner's (1994) study of innovation in row 4. The authors report a marginally significant *positive* association between works council presence and their innovation measure. Interestingly, however, this result is highly sensitive to that other indicator of workplace representation, union density. That is, after some level of workplace organization any benefits of works council presence are lost. This tipping point occurs at a union density of 51 percent. Once this threshold is breached, the positive impact of the works council is reversed and the association becomes increasingly negative.

Row 5 summarizes results for the only study to investigate investment in tangible capital. In their analysis of the determinants of the ratio of gross capital formation to the capital stock in some 50 manufacturing establishments in 2 German *Länder* in 1990/91, Addison, Kraft, and Wagner (1993) find that plants with works councils undertake significantly less investment than their counterparts without works councils. That said, there are no signs that this negative association is replicated in the cases of the two other output indicators—value-added and pretax profits—identified in this study.

Generally insignificant associations between works council presence and a subjective measure(s) of profitability, as well as a measure of product innovation, are reported by Addison and Wagner (1997) in their study of 175 industrial firms in Lower Saxony in 1993 (row 6 of the table). Addison and Wagner also attempt to capture the impact of the degree of influence wielded by the works council. They derive an *index of works council voice* according to the reported involvement of the entity in four areas of decision making. A marginally significant negative association is found between the extent of works council voice and the achievement of high profitability, again as assessed by the manager respondent. By contrast, the coefficient estimates for a conventional works council dummy variable are statistically insignificant throughout, irrespective of whether or not works council presence is endogenized.

The penultimate study in row 7 of table 4.1 is noteworthy for its attempt to inquire into the black box of mechanisms through which works councils are supposed to achieve the benefits commonly attributed to them. In his study of quits, Kraft (1986) pools two years of data on metalworking firms (i.e., the same sample as subsequently used by FitzRoy and Kraft in the studies summarized in the first two rows of the table). His dependent variable is a dummy variable capturing low/ high turnover among unskilled workers. This measure is based on a question inquiring of the manager-respondents whether the quit rates of unskilled workers were either "high" or "low."[4] The variable is then regressed on an index of *individual voice*, works council presence (the proxy for collective voice), union density, the average wage, the percentage of blue-collar workers, per capita training expenditures, firm size, and variables capturing production techniques and organization structure (flow production and the number of workers per foreman, respectively), and a share ownership dummy equal to one if top management owns at least one-quarter of the firms equity. The novel individual voice argument is constructed on the basis of replies to questions as to "the decision possibilities of blue-collar workers on investment and rationalization, coordination of work groups and other personnel decisions, and the determination of (individual) job design" (Kraft, 1986, p. 702).

Kraft's single-equation estimates indicate that turnover is materially reduced the greater the opportunities for the exercise of individual voice. In contrast, the coefficient estimate for collective voice/works council presence is positive but not statistically significant. All the remaining covariates are shown to have effects on turnover as might be expected on human capital and organizational grounds, inter alia.[5]

Since employees with high tenure may be granted more decision rights (or, alternatively, firms might use individual voice to lower turnover), Kraft also estimates a simultaneous equation probit model of the determinants of high quit rates and of decision rights or voice. His basic single-equation findings hold up very well. Indeed, the coefficient estimate on voice in the quit equation increases in absolute magnitude, while the quit variable is not statistically significant in the voice equation. In short, no feedback effects from quits to voice are discernible in the data. Also as before, neither unions nor works councils influence quits one way or another.

The final study by FitzRoy and Kraft (1995) in table 4.1 is an exercise on the choice of incentive payment systems in firms according to technology and other, usually unobserved parameters. Here the authors are less concerned with the effects of works councils than with the biases that result from not allowing for the fact that firms select into either individual or group incentive schemes. Thus, for example, those firms that choose *not* to introduce profit sharing do so for profit-maximizing reasons: they would be disadvantaged had they done so.

Alternatively put, they have a comparative advantage in deploying *individual* incentives. Since in their row 2 study the authors report a positive effect of profit sharing on total factor productivity, but do not control for the endogeneity of payment systems, the possibility arises that the earlier results provide an upwardly biased estimate of the potential gains to the generality of firms from operating those schemes.

FitzRoy and Kraft do indeed find this to be the case. But for us the more striking result is that the coefficient estimate for the works council dummy is positive and statistically significant in the selectivity adjusted value-added equation for firms operating profit sharing schemes but not for those without profit sharing schemes (where the works council coefficient is now negative and statistically significant). The authors conclude that the former result points to cooperative labor relations.

4.4   Interpretation

Our reading of the first phase of econometric research into the operation of German works councils leads frankly to a somewhat pessimistic view of the entity. After all, we have reported evidence of negative associations between works council presence and productivity, profitability, innovation, and (in one case) investment in physical capital. Nor is there any indication that they reduce quits, although it will be recalled that the dependent variable in this particular case was a dummy variable. Ultimately, works councils appear as constraints. But if works councils appear as *impedimenta* rather than active pecuniary rent seekers, there is virtually nothing positive to report about their impact in the early economic literature.[6] That main exception, as we have just seen, pertains to profit sharing. Although works councils do not seem to actually promote profit sharing, there is some indication that they may have a positive effect on value-added in firms covered by profit sharing. So they are seemingly not inimical to cooperative labor relations.

But the literature we have reviewed is not without blemish. One immediate cause of concern is the issue of sample size. Now the use of small samples should reduce the precision of the works council coefficient estimate and thus predispose any test against finding a works council effect. But the main issue here is the very representativeness of the negative findings. In other words, are they likely to carry over to the generality of industrial firms in Germany?

The cross-section nature of the studies is a further complicating factor, and is aggravated by the limited number of control variables in some of the studies. Causation is a thorny problem and is tackled using systems of equations in the majority of the studies. But there is the standard problem of identifying the simultaneous equations (e.g., identifying and measuring factors that influence works council presence but not, say, productivity). And in the most sophisticated studies reviewed here in which exogenous productivity (i.e., as estimated without the influence—negative in this case—of works councils on productivity) is directly associated with works council election, reverse causality can still apply. An additional concern is that omitted determinants of productivity may be correlated with the works council variable leading us to mistakenly attribute to works councils the impact of some omitted factor. As was hinted at above, one solution to this problem is through the inclusion of a detailed set of control variables in all equations. Ultimately, however, the solution resides in the use of longitudinal data (see the studies reviewed in chapter 6 in particular).

Another issue concerns the works council variable. As we have seen, the above studies typically recoup the works council effect from the coefficient estimate for actual or predicted works council presence. An immediate concern is that, as we have seen from chapter 2, most establishments over a certain size (500 employees) have works councils, while most plants under a certain size (21 employees) do not. In other words, over certain ranges of employment one cannot hope to identify a works council effect using a measure based on presence of the entity alone. (The competence of the works council is also increasing in establishment size, which is a further complication.) Accordingly, one should use samples containing a goodly number of establishments with and without works councils. Moreover, whatever the general disadvantage of small samples of firms from the perspective of statistical inference, observe that some of the data sets of this phase of the literature have been rich enough to allow the researcher to fashion measures of the degree of involvement of the works council in decision making (the row 6 study) or to examine the relationship between the works council and workplace union density (rows 3 and 4).

Finally, observe that not all performance outcomes have received equal treatment in this phase of the literature. For example, there is a seeming neglect of employment indicators. Even if it is a more ambiguous performance measure than some other indicators[7] (e.g., labor productivity) just one of the early studies examines employment (row 7). And this study is unconventional in focusing *force majeure* on a subjective measure of quits rather than an objective, continuous measure of turnover. However, the use of a subjective indicator can be informative.

First, objective data may not be available for individual skill categories. Second, absent formalization of what constitutes an optimal quit rate, a manager's identification of "excessive" quits, or lack thereof, might usefully supplement objective data; in particular, indications of higher quit rates in plants without works councils may have no implications for efficiency when subjective data fail to identify turnover as problematic or "high."

In sum, despite some real data strengths—including in some cases rather detailed information on establishment variables—and insights, the fact remains that the findings of the early research literature may not be representative by reason of sample size, and sector and region covered. As a result, the associations uncovered cannot be generalized beyond the samples investigated. Nevertheless, the studies offer important guidelines for future research while at the same time suggesting some potentially important innovative lines of inquiry. Among the latter are the union-works council nexus, the role of different "types" of works councils, and the covariation between works councils and innovative work practices.

CHAPTER 5

The Emergence of a More Positive View of Workplace Codetermination: Evidence from Some Larger Datasets

5.1 Introduction

Studies in the next phase of econometric research were able to draw on large-scale data sets, principally the Hanover Firm Panel (*Hannoveraner Firmenpanel*) and the NIFA-(*Neue Informationstechnologien und Flexible Arbeitssysteme/New Information Technologies and Flexible Work* Systems) Panel. The population of the first data set is all manufacturing establishments with at least five employees in the state of Lower Saxony. The actual sample of plants is stratified according to firm size and industry. It comprises 1,025 establishments in 1994, declining to 709 establishments by the time of the fourth and final wave in 1997 because of sample attrition (for a description of this data set, see Brand, Carstensen, Gerlach, and Klodt, 1996; Gerlach, Hübler, and Meyer, 2003). The second survey covers all establishments with 20 or more employees in the German machine tool industry. This panel has eight waves, 1991–1998. The sample base is approximately 6,000 companies, and the realized sample ranges from a maximum of 1,642 in the first year to a minimum of 1,038 in the last year (see Schmidt and Widmaier, 1992; Widmaier, 2001). One advantage of the NIFA-Panel is that it allows for differentiation between "types" of works councils on the basis management assessment of their "attitude" (see below).[1] Unfortunately, this question was only asked in the 1996 wave.

There is also a third data set in the form of a nationally representative but older, employment-based survey of 2,392 private sector firms employing at least five employees from the industrial and service sectors conducted by Büchtemann and Höland (1989) in 1987 to evaluate the effects of the German Employment Promotion Act (*Arbeitsförderungsgesetz*) of 1985. Reflecting its narrower focus on employment issues, use of this data set has been restricted to the analysis of labor fluctuations.

As we shall see, the overall view of works council impact reported in studies using these larger data sets is rather more favorable than before. The jury is still out on how much of this difference reflects the unrepresentativeness of the earlier research as opposed to, say, the improvement in, or maturation of, the relationship between firms and their works councils flagged in the German industrial relations literature (see Kotthoff, 1994). But more important, however, are the new themes opened up by this Phase 2 literature.

5.2 Themes

At the price of some imprecision, we can identify four main distinguishing characteristics of the new research literature. Beginning with the most general theme, there is first a tendency to look for differences in works council impact by establishment size. There are several reasons for this. One is the point made earlier that very large plants almost always have works councils while small plants seldom do. Another reason is that works council competence or authority (number of councilors, number of paid councilors, entitlements to information and consultation, and input in matters of personnel selection, etc.) is as a matter of law increasing in establishment size (chapter 2). When a dummy variable capturing the presence or otherwise of a works council at the establishment is used in a regression model, lacking information on works council type (but see section 5.3) the variable can best pick up the effect of the institution if there is a fair representation of firms in both categories (i.e., with and without a council) and where the rights of the works council are a datum (the same for all establishments). If only a tiny number of firms in a sample have/do not have a council, we cannot expect to be able to estimate the effect of the entity with any precision. And if the legal rights of a council are not held constant over the establishments in the sample, a simple dummy variable cannot, as a matter of construction, take care of this variation and any related variation in the economic impact of works councils in firms of different size. In this light, some of the studies examined here seek to estimate the association between works councils and various performance outcomes by looking at firms with between 21 and 100 employees, where both restrictions are met. A separate and more general size-related issue is that there are practical grounds for believing that the costs of the code-termination apparatus may be greater and the benefits smaller for specific categories of plant.

Second, turning to more specific concerns, greater attention is paid in the new literature to labor turnover issues. As we saw in chapter 4 just one of the small-sample studies tackled the turnover issue. But the voice aspects of the institution coupled with its design features (e.g., intention to promote trustful and cooperative industrial relations) justify more attention being given over to labor turnover. Potentially less positive aspects of works council operation stemming from bargaining power transcend the turnover issue and there has been some recent consideration of their effect on employment growth using the Hanover Firm Panel.

Third, an intriguing new development has been the inclusion in the developing literature of a collective bargaining variable proper. Unlike the earlier studies reviewed in chapter 4, the large-scale data sets of this phase of the econometric literature either lack reliable information on union density or contain no information on it at all. Reflecting the dual system of industrial relations in Germany, some of the new studies instead use the presence or otherwise of a framework collective bargaining agreement at regional or industry level.[2]

This particular development was spearheaded by Hübler and Jirjahn (2003), who seek to test Freeman and Lazear's (1995) argument that where a works council is embedded in an external collective bargaining framework this will serve to dissipate distributional squabbles at the workplace, thereby enhancing any pro-productive effect of the works council (see also chapter 3).

Hübler and Jirjahn characterize the dual system via a three-stage game. In the first stage, the employer decides on whether or not to join an employer association. There are costs of doing so. Apart from membership dues, there is also the issue of the constraints that membership places upon the flexibility of the firm. But wage costs are discounted on the practical ground that collectively agreed wages are generalized throughout the system (both formally and informally) and, more importantly, because the model presupposes that coverage will have a moderating effect on wages by restraining the rent-seeking activities of works councils. At the second stage, workers for their part decide on establishing a works council. There are costs attached to this strategy in the form of coordination and communication costs. Finally, in the third stage, output is produced and additional bargaining may occur if a council is established.

Strictly speaking, the game-theoretic setup is illustrative. The empirical contribution of the authors is to allow for the correlation between the disturbance terms in equations modeling works council presence and coverage by a collective agreement. Thence the selectivity terms (obtained from maximum likelihood univariate and bivariate probit estimates of works council presence and collective bargaining coverage) are included in wage and productivity outcome equations for all establishments taken as a whole and, in the preferred specification, for separate subsamples of establishments with and without collective agreements. Again, the underlying voice model recognizes that works councils have two faces. The benign face fosters trust and cooperation and provides a mechanism for negotiating productivity-enhancing work practices. The other, bargaining face may hinder decision making if the two sides fail to reach agreement and result in the negotiation of less productive work practices that require lower effort levels *and* raise wages. Formally, works councils weaken management's disagreement position, so that the maintained hypothesis is that management's disagreement position is weakened less if the establishment is covered by a collective agreement. Employers' associations, so the argument runs, support management with expertise in case there are lawsuits, narrowing the opportunities for a works council to obtain wage increases.[3]

Further, Hübler and Jirjahn argue that unions are also interested in preventing works councils from rent seeking since plant level bargaining undercuts union power and status while contributing to widened earnings dispersion across firms (see chapter 6). The authors also note in this regard that the union interest transcends that of the workforce in an individual establishment. This wider interest may at least in part be reflected in the objective function of the works council. For all these reasons, Hübler and Jirjahn (2003, p. 472) conclude that "the presence of works councils should have a more substantial impact on productivity and a less intense impact on wages in the covered industrial relations regime."

The notion that strong collective bargaining can be beneficial is also encountered in Britain, where it has been argued that unions need to be strong if they are to be effective agents of collective voice (see Bryson, 2004b). In the German case, as we have seen, the argument is particularly interesting because of the prospect of a (potential) decoupling of distribution from production issues.[4]

This brings us to the fourth and final theme of the new literature based on large samples of firms, namely, the inclusion of arguments covering employee involvement mechanisms/high performance work practices (Addison, 2005). The bridging link between the studies of the first phase of research and the material of this second phase is the follow-up study by FitzRoy and Kraft (1995) in which the authors qualified their harsh interpretation of works council impact on establishment performance in finding evidence of a well-determined *positive* association between works councils and productivity in profit sharing regimes (see chapter 4).[5] But the new literature breaks new ground in examining a wider range of employee involvement mechanisms/high performance workplace practices (including profit sharing schemes for managers) than heretofore, and in investigating the role of the "engagement" of the works council.

5.3 Findings

In table 5.1 we provide results from a representative but not exhaustive set of studies covering the research themes identified earlier, which we will supplement as appropriate with other studies from this phase of the research literature.[6] Beginning with labor turnover, the findings reported at various points in the table are seemingly at odds with results from the sole Phase 1 study. As can be seen in row 1 of the table, Frick and Sadowski (1995), using data from the Büchtemann and Höland (1989) data set, report that both quits and dismissals are materially reduced in the presence of works councils.[7]

Although data from the much richer Hanover Firm Panel do not always point to reduced separations in works council regimes—while also indicating that management in works council plants is more prone to complain that employment levels are excessive (on which more below)—they tend to tell much the same employment story. Thus, for example, Addison, Schnabel, and Wagner (2001) find that hires, separations, and dismissals are all reduced in works council settings, other than in the case of smaller establishments with 21–100 employees (row 2). The same tendency is evident in Dilger's (2002) analysis of personnel fluctuation using the NIFA-Panel (row 6).[8]

Since lower quit rates increase the time horizon over which training investments may be recouped, they imply greater training. In a comparatively recent study using the Hanover Firm Panel that is not summarized in table 5.1, Gerlach and Jirjahn (2001) report that works council

Table 5.1 The Economic Impact of the Works Council—Phase 2 Studies

Study	Data	Dependent Variable(s)	Methodology	Findings
1. Frick and Sadowski (1995)[a]	1,616 firms taken from a nationally representative survey of 2,392 for-profit enterprises in the manufacturing and service sectors. Data cover the period May 1985–April 1987.	Quit and dismissal rates.	Single-equation log-odds model estimated by OLS.	Works council presence associated with statistically significant reductions in quits and dismissals (2.4 and 2.9 percentage points, respectively).
2. Addison, Schnabel, and Wagner (2001)[b]	c. 900 establishments from the 1994 wave of the Hanover Firm Panel (see text). Detailed establishment and industry controls.	Value-added per worker; subjective measure(s) of financial performance; wages and salaries per employee (and the percentage "wage gap"); three labor turnover measures (hires, separations, and gross turnover); and two measures of innovation (introduction of new processes/products).	Single-equation estimates. Separate results for all establishments and a subset of plants with 21–100 employees.	Works council presence associated with higher labor productivity overall, but not for establishments with 21–100 employees. Profitability systematically lower in the presence of works councils. Wages are higher when there are works councils but the sources of these higher earnings are not transparent. All labor turnover measures are reduced in the presence of works councils other than for the subset of smaller establishments. Neither process nor product innovation is materially influenced by works council presence.

58

Study	Data	Dependent variable	Method	Findings
3. Hübler and Jirjahn (2003)	Pooled data from the 1994 and 1996 waves of the Hanover Firm Panel (see text). Detailed establishment and industry controls, including whether or not the plant is covered by an (external) collective agreement.	Value added per worker, and wages and salaries per employee.	Bivariate probit maximum likelihood estimates of works council presence and coverage by a collective agreement to form selection arguments in the outcome equations.	Positive effect of works council on productivity measure is statistically significant only where the plant is covered by a collective agreement with and without selectivity correction into works council and collective bargaining status. But wages are higher in works council regimes in wage equations estimated across covered and uncovered establishments.
4. Jirjahn (2003b)	As above. Detailed establishment and industry controls, including whether or not plant management covered by a profit sharing arrangement.	Value-added per employee.	Single-equation OLS model (auxiliary probit model of works council presence provided, but not used to provide selectivity-adjusted estimates). Separate estimates for all establishments and a subset of plants with 21–100 employees.	Across all establishments and the subset of smaller plants, the effect of works council presence is positive and statistically significant (in all but one specification). Executive profit sharing schemes are also pro-productive throughout, although the interaction effect is negative and significant for the all-establishment case.
5. Wagner, Schank, Schnabel, and Addison (2006)	691 plants from the 1994 wave of the Hanover Firm Panel. Detailed set of regressors including a quadratic in establishment size, branch plant status, proportions of part-timers, females, and blue-collar/highly educated employees,	Value added per employee.	Quantile regression methods. Results presented for 0.10, 0.25, 0.50, 0.75, and 0.90 quantiles.	The positive and statistically significant coefficient estimate for the works council dummy estimated in benchmark OLS vanishes for large parts of the distribution. Such an effect can only be detected in plants (the overachievers) at the top end of the conditional productivity distribution,

Continued

Table 5.1 Continued

Study	Data	Dependent variable(s)	Methodology	Findings
	modernity of human capital stock, degree of capacity utilization, length of working week, presence of shiftworking, market share.			contrary to the managerial competence hypothesis.
6. Frick (2001)	c. 1,700 establishments from the sixth (1996) wave of the NIFA-Panel. This data set identifies five high performance work practices (HPWP). It also distinguishes five types of works council as assessed by management (ranging from "antagonistic" to "excluded") and a variable identifying greater involvement of the works council in processes of technological and/or organizational change than laid down under the law or collective agreements.	Number of HPWP practices.	Descriptive analysis: gives number of HPWP used in plants by works council presence, involvement, and type. The five HPWP are reductions in hierarchies, delegation of decision making, work groups with independent budgets, group or teamwork, and flexible working time. Multiple classification analysis: uses same categories as for descriptive treatment and five covariates (viz. log number of employees, log sales per employee, stock of orders, and the degrees of capacity and manpower utilization).	Establishments with works councils use more HPWP than plants without works councils, although this difference is not statistically significant in the multivariate analysis. Establishments with works council involvement in technological and organizational change exceeding that set down by law or collective agreement also have more HPWP than do plants with less involved councils. But the number of HPWP is highest in establishments where the works council is rated "antagonistic." HPWP are reported to have a positive effect on establishment performance but a negative influence on labor demand.

| 7. Dilger (2002) | NIFA-Panel, as above, but supplemented with information on works council presence from the fourth (1994) wave. Three works council measures identified: a simple dummy variable indicating presence or otherwise of the entity, a set of dummy variables for the various types of works councils (see row 5 above), and the change in works council status, 1994–1996. Detailed establishment level controls. | Quit, hire, and labor fluctuation rates; flexible working time; product innovation; and financial performance (a dummy variable indicating the achievement of at least a "sufficient" rate of return). | Single-equation cross-section OLS regressions for departure, hire, and labor fluctuation rates. Single-equation, cross-section logit models for flexible working time, product innovation, and financial performance. Models for flexible working time, product innovation, and profitability are also estimated separately for plants with 21–100 employees. Multinomial logit models for the determinants of flexible working time use the three works council measures and detailed plant level controls. | Works councils consistently reduce all measures of personnel fluctuation, but the coefficient estimates for some types of works councils are not statistically significant at conventional levels. Works councils promote the use of flexible working time (in both the all-establishment sample and the subset of plants with 21–100 employees), but the effects by type of council are not always well determined. Although works councils do not in general influence product innovation, where their involvement in technological and organizational changes exceeds that laid down by law or collective agreement the effect is positive and weakly statistically significant. The impact of works councils on financial performance is negative for all establishments and smaller establishments, but is not statistically significant where the degree of engagement of the council in technological/organizational change exceeds benchmark levels. |

Continued

61

Table 5.1 Continued

Study	Data	Dependent variable(s)	Methodology	Findings
8. Jirjahn (2008b)	602 firms from the Hanover Firm Panel, 1994–1997. Detailed establishment level controls plus 18 industry group dummies.	Employment growth (two measures: annual rate of employment change and change in employment divided by average employment), works council presence in auxiliary equation.	OLS regression model plus treatment effects maximum likelihood model plus two-step IV regression model estimated by 2SLS.	Single-equation estimates point to a positive but statistically insignificant association between works council presence and employment growth. Taking the endogeneity of works councils into account yields a highly significant positive relation between works council presence and employment growth. Specifically, establishments with works councils have 7 percentage point higher growth per year than their counterparts without works councils. In establishments also covered by a collective agreement, the overall effect is a 5 percentage point employment growth advantage. Basic idea is that employee interest in forming a works council depends on factors that negatively impact employment growth.

[a] See also Backes-Gellner, Frick, and Sadowski (1997); Frick (1996); Frick (1997).
[b] See also Addison, Siebert, Wagner (1996, 1998); Addison, Siebert, Wagner, and Wei (2001).

presence is positively correlated with further training investments. (Other correlates of training in this study are establishment size, the qualification level of the workforce, the use of advanced technology, and other forms of participative work organization.) Any such training effect had hitherto been *surmised* from the evidence on quit rates and dismissals (e.g., Backes-Gellner, Frick, and Sadowski, 1997). We shall chart further progress in analyzing works council "effects" on training in chapter 6 on the basis of matched employer-employee data.[9]

We will return to the wider issue of labor adjustment at the conclusion of our discussion. Meantime, we consider the issue of works council impact by collective bargaining regime. The study in row 3 of the table offers the first test of Freeman and Lazear's (1995) argument that, where a works council is embedded in an external collective bargaining framework, this will serve to dissipate distributional squabbles at the workplace, thereby enhancing any pro-productive effect of the works council. Hübler and Jirjahn (2003) test the model using pooled data from two waves of the Hanover Firm Panel. Both works council presence and collective bargaining coverage are treated as endogenous and modeled in separate productivity and wage equations. The authors' main estimates are for separate wage and productivity equations by collective bargaining status. The productivity results in particular offer support for the model: labor productivity is higher in works council regimes but only where the establishment is covered by a collective agreement. The wage results are somewhat less compelling. That is to say, the idea that collective agreements can police rent-seeking behavior is undercut by the finding of higher wages in all works council establishments in some specifications.[10]

The studies in rows 2 and 5 of the table, each drawing on the first wave of the Hanover Firm Panel, again suggest that works councils may be associated with greater labor productivity. But Addison, Schnabel, and Wagner's (2001) simple OLS estimates suggest that the positive association between works council presence and value added per employee is confined to larger establishments. Using more sophisticated methods, Wagner, Schank, Schnabel, and Addison (2006) report that the impact of works councils on labor productivity varies along the conditional distribution of value added per employee. The authors' quantile regression analysis indicates that positive effects can only be detected at the top end of that distribution. Thus, in a seeming reversal of the managerial competence model, highly competent managers may be able to cooperate with works councils in a way that enhances productivity.

This brings us to the fourth theme of the new literature: the inclusion of employee involvement mechanisms and so-called high performance work practices. The two main studies covering employee involvement/high performance work practices are reported in rows 6 and 7 of table 5.1. But we should preface our review of this material with some remarks on the study in row 4 of the table that focuses on the interaction between works councils and profit sharing schemes for *managers*. In his analysis of two waves of data from the Hanover Firm Panel, Jirjahn (2003b) finds that the positive association between works councils and labor productivity is strengthened after allowing for management incentive schemes that are themselves pro-productive. As shown in the table, he also reports that the coefficient estimate for the interaction term between the two is negative and statistically significant,[11] which the author interprets as consistent with either of two hypotheses: either profit sharing management reduces the commitment value of agency in circumstances where the works council cannot foster trust and loyalty absent the cooperation of management, or management rent seeking is curbed by profit sharing and the works council is not so important for building cooperation in situations of reduced opportunism on the part of management. We shall review the agency and contract-theoretic basis of this interesting study in greater detail in chapter 7. Suffice it to say here that although its findings are ultimately inconclusive—specifically as regards the contention that works councils may play a particularly important role for the economic success of the establishment when no managerial profit sharing is in place—the emphasis placed on the managerial environment in this study is a welcome addition to the theoretical literature.

The two penultimate studies in table 5.1 return us to the issue of nonexecutive employee involvement mechanisms/high performance workplace practices. Each exploits the NIFA-Panel for the machine tool industry. This data set is of interest for three main reasons. First, as noted in section 5.2, its sixth wave contains management's assessment of the working relationship with the works council. Specifically, the NIFA survey asks the management respondent to rate the works council entity as (1) "mostly antagonistic," (2) "sometimes difficult," (3) "unreservedly cooperative," (4) "passive," and (5) "excluded by management." Second, it identifies a set of five employee involvement mechanisms/high performance workplace practices. Third, the data set also records additional information on the degree of engagement (i.e., involvement) of the works council.

It can be seen from the table that the results of using this additional material are mixed. Thus, the study by Frick (2001) in row 6 finds that firms with works councils tend to use more high performance workplace practices than their counterparts without works councils, but that the number of such practices is highest where the institution is dubbed "antagonistic" by management. More positively, it can be seen from Dilger's (2002) wider-ranging study, summarized in row 7 of the table, that although the general tendency is for works council plants to record lower profitability—a result based on a subjective measure of returns that is consistently reported for the Hanover Firm Panel as well (see the row 2 entry and the other references footnoted there)—this effect can apparently be negated by greater works council involvement. In addition, some beneficial effect of the works council on product innovation is detected in circumstances where its degree of engagement is above normal.

The final study in row 8 of table 5.1 returns us to the important issue of employment effects with which we began this empirical discussion. In one sense the study by Jirjahn (2008) is intended as a reply to other employment growth studies of the most recent phase of research that we shall evaluate in chapter 7. We consider it here because of its basis in the Hanover Firm Panel.

The study offers a straight forward treatment of employment growth in manufacturing industry in Lower Saxony over the interval 1994–1997. Its innovation resides in the attempt control for works council endogeneity.[12] Specifically, Jirjahn argues that the effect of works councils on employment change is biased in OLS estimation because there are factors negatively associated with employment growth that are positively associated with the existence of a works council; in particular, workers are supposed to elect a council when the establishment is facing a long-term crisis. In his treatment-effects model (later supplemented with a standard IV approach) identification is achieved by nonlinearity plus a single exclusion restriction: the presence of active owners within the establishment. This variable enters the works council equation but not the employment change equation. Active managers, so the argument runs, are meant to stimulate works council formation but not employment growth. Joint estimation of the works council and employment growth equations reveals negative correlation between the error terms in both equations. As compared with the OLS results, the coefficient estimate for the works council variable abruptly increases in magnitude from 0.0091 and statistically insignificant to 0.0702 and statistically significant at the 0.01 level. In other words, works councils raise employment growth by no less than 7 percentage points—at a time when employment is shrinking on average. Further, the author reports that these results are robust to an alternative measure of employment growth, to plant size (a subsample of establishments with 21–200 employees, which note crosses an authority threshold), and to the inclusion of additional covariates.

Overall, this review of the second phase of research ends with a bang, not a whimper.[13] More conservatively, with the main exception of the profits result (see rows 2 and 6), works council "effects" emerge as either benign or potentially pro-productive.

5.4   Concluding Remarks

Even if they contain few if any technical innovations, the studies of this second phase of research are noteworthy for their creative use of both existing and new variables such as establishment size, collective bargaining, and employee involvement. To repeat, the use of these variables in performance equations has revealed the works council institution in more favorable light than the studies of the first phase of research. As cases in point, recall the findings that works councils may be associated with higher productivity (least controversially perhaps in larger plants); that the dual industrial relations system may allow the pro-productive potential of works councils to be realized; and that works council effects along a number of performance dimensions may be positive when taken in conjunction with other forms of employee involvement. To be sure, there remain a number of inconsistencies and ambiguities in the literature. One such example is the nagging issue of establishment profitability. Nearly every study points to poorer financial performance in works council regimes, but what is the source of this deficit if, as is seemingly the case, (higher) wages and (lower) productivity do not emerge as consistent culprits, even if the former contention has to be carefully qualified?[14] Another example is employee involvement. Are employee involvement and other workplace practices complements or substitutes for works councils? The literature tilts toward acceptance of complementarity, but the issue is not settled given the negative and statistically significant correlation association between teamworking and works council presence in the Hanover Firm Panel (see, in particular, Addison, Schnabel, and Wagner, 1997).

Almost all the research summarized in this chapter is cross-sectional. Problems of statistical inference may arise if the determinants of the key independent variable—works council presence (type, or intensity)—are not accounted for. For example, works councils may be introduced in circumstances of economic difficulty *or* advantage. Also, their introduction may reflect unobserved differences in the costs and benefits of the institution at plant level that may in turn be linked to the outcomes in which we are interested. As in the earlier literature, there have been some attempts to endogenize works councils presence, although identification is particularly difficult in this case. Further, if some permanent unobserved plant characteristic is associated with both works council presence and the outcome indicator, accounting for the nonrandom distribution of the works council with a cross-section will not suffice. In short, biases may attach to these estimates, and causality continues to be an issue. A final question is whether the above findings are representative given the regional and industrial composition *and vintage* of the two main data sets examined here. This is the issue of external validity. Fortunately, in each of the above respects this is not the end of the story, because economists now have access to an unambiguously nationally representative data set with a truly longitudinal capacity. It is toward an examination of research based on this data set that we next turn.

CHAPTER 6

The Impact of Workplace Codetermination: Findings from the Third Phase of Research

6.1 Introduction

In this chapter we review findings from the most recent phase of German research into the impact of works councils. Since the hallmark of this research is the use of large data sets, we shall begin with a brief descriptive statement of this material. We next present the evidence along three main dimensions: "standard" performance outcomes (productivity, investment, and employment); employee/involvement high performance work practices and their relationship with works councils; and wage effects. In our concluding remarks we draw together the threads of the preceding arguments, comment on a new line of post–works council research, and sketch some topics of future inquiry.

6.2 Data Sources

The two main data sets used by researchers in Phase 3 are the Establishment Panel (*Betriebspanel*) of the Institute for Labor Market Research (*Institut für Arbeitsmarkt- und Berufsforschung/IAB*) of the Federal Labor Agency (*Bundesagentur für Arbeit*) and the IAB Linked Employer-Employee data set, or LIAB. A secondary data set, used in some of the most recent wage studies, is the Structure of Earnings Survey (*Gehalts- und Lohnstrukturerhebung*), or GSES. We briefly describe each in turn.

Beginning in 1993 the IAB Establishment Panel has surveyed several thousand establishments from all sectors of the economy in the former West Germany and, since 1996, for the unified Germany. The

Establishment Panel is based on a stratified random sample—the strata are for 17 industries[1] and 10 employment size classes—from the population of all establishments with at least one employee covered by social insurance (see Kölling, 2000; Bellmann, Kohaut, and Lahner, 2002; Fischer, Janik, Müller, and Schmucker, 2008). To correct for panel mortality, exits, and newly founded units, the data are augmented regularly. Familiarly, the data are collected in personal interviews with the owner or senior management of the establishment. The purpose of the panel is to serve the needs of the Federal Labor Agency—as well as to provide a national employer survey for scientific analysis—and so its focus is employment-related matters such as labor turnover, level and composition of employment, apprenticeship training, investments, and subsidies. The survey is conducted in mid-year and as a result some questions (e.g., annual sales, investment, and the profit situation) are asked retrospectively in the following year's survey. Today, approximately 16,000 establishments are surveyed annually.

From time to time additional questions are added to the survey. Examples include questions on employee share ownership and profit sharing, teamworking, devolved decision making, as well as additional information on training and the goals of training programs—all of which as we shall see have variously been used to identify employee involvement/high performance work practices.[2] Among the most recent such additions is a question dealing with the cooperativeness or otherwise of the works council (although only for 2006 thus far). Note that since 2002 the more routine question on the presence of a works council has been asked every year. Prior to that it was asked of all establishments only in 1993, 1996, 1998, and 2000 with interpolations for 1997, 1999, and 2001 being provided by the IAB (though the question has always been asked of panel accessions). Information on the collective bargaining coverage of the establishment has been available since 1995. Finally, since 2003 but not in every year there has been a question on alternative forms of worker representation.

The second data set used in the wage studies reviewed in this chapter is intimately related to the former. The linked employer-employee data set of the IAB, or LIAB, is created by matching the data of the IAB Establishment Panel with Federal Employment Agency employment statistics. The employment statistics are drawn from the German *Employment Statistics Register*, an administrative panel data set of all employees paying social security contributions (see Bender, Haas, and Klose, 2000; Alda, Bender, Gartner, 2005). It covers more than 98 percent of the employees (and trainees) included in the Establishment

Panel. The employment register was set up in 1973 to integrate the notification procedures for social security pensions, health insurance, and unemployment insurance. Information is recorded at the start and end of the individual's employment spell with the firm and in annual end-year reports. The LIAB currently covers the period 1975–2005, but is continuously updated. The employment statistics contain data on the individual's three-digit occupation, five-digit industry, gross daily wage up to the earnings ceiling for social security contributions, gender, year of birth, nationality, marital status, number of children, and schooling/training. Both the wage and tenure data are top coded, so that both have to be imputed when estimating conventional earnings functions. The data also include the individual's establishment number. This number serves as a definition criterion for the establishment, as a selection basis for the IAB Establishment Panel, and of course for the linking of the employee and establishment data.

Finally, the German Structure of Earnings Survey is a cross-sectional linked employer-employee data set (Hafner, 2004). The sample (of around 850,000 employees) includes in addition to workers in regular employment, employees in vocational training, and those in marginal employment and in partial retirement schemes. A clear advantage of this data set, at least since 2001, is that the wage information is not censored as in the LIAB. A disadvantage is that there is no information on whether the worker is covered by a works council. On the other hand, the survey provides firm level information on collective bargaining coverage (either firm or sectoral) and also gives each individual worker's coverage status.

6.3 Literature Review

In reviewing the modern literature, we propose to present the evidence in three parts. The first will consider the standard performance arguments of productivity, investment, and employment (broadly interpreted). The second part will focus on innovative work practices and, where possible, their relation to works councils. The final component tackles the measured effect of works councils on wages and will revisit our earlier discussion of the works council-collective bargaining nexus.

6.3.1 Works Councils, Productivity, Investment, and Employment

Table 6.1A provides a snapshot of the more recent research into the effect of works councils on productivity, investment, and various aspects of employment using the IAB Establishment Panel. (The works council-productivity nexus will receive further scrutiny in table 6.1B in the context of employee involvement/high performance work practices.) The study summarized in the first row of the table points to a strong positive association between works council presence and economic performance. Frick and Möller's (2003) production function estimates update the formal production function studies first estimated over small samples of firms in Phase 1 of the literature (see the studies by FitzRoy and Kraft, 1987, and Addison, Kraft and Wagner, 1993, in rows 2 and 5 of table 4.1). The authors use the question in the Establishment Panel asking for information on "replacement investment" (i.e., depreciation) as a rough proxy for the capital stock. Their works-council-in-the-production-function estimates suggest that labor productivity is as much as 25–30 percent higher in works council regimes. (Supportive results, albeit of somewhat lesser magnitude are reported by Wolf and Zwick [2002, 2008] in a study summarized in table 6.1B, below).

In contrast to the above, each of the two other production function studies contained in table 6.1A suggest that establishments with and without a works council do *not* exhibit statistically significant differences in efficiency from one another. We note parenthetically that each study substitutes sales for value-added because of the large number of missing values on materials cost in the IAB Firm Panel.[3] In the row 2 study, Schank, Schnabel, and Wagner (2002) estimate separate fixed effects frontier production functions for work council and nonworks council regimes, and then compare the technical efficiencies of median plants in the two workplace regimes. Only plants with between 21 and 100 employees (throughout the period 1993–2000) are sampled as a rough control for works council heterogeneity—it will be recalled that the powers of the work council are a datum over this size interval—and also to maintain a good mix of both types of workplace regime in the sample (recall that very large plants almost always have a works council while very small plants seldom do). The confidence intervals of the reported technical efficiency estimates for the two types of plants overlap, leading the authors to conclude that there is no evidence that works council plants are any more efficient than their works council-free counterparts.

The study by Addison, Schank, Schnabel, and Wagner (2006) in row 3 of the table gets the Frick-Möller result in regressions using pooled data—namely, a works council "effect" of around 25 percent—but reports that this strong pro-productivity effect is sensitive to

Table 6.1A The Economic Impact of the Works Council on Productivity, Investment, and Employment—Phase 3 Studies

Study	Data	Dependent Variable(s)	Methodology	Findings
1. Frick and Möller (2003)[a]	IAB Establishment Panel, using cross-sections for 1998 and 2000 with 1,770 (2,434) observations for western (eastern) Germany.	Log value-added.	A works-council-in-the-production-function test (Cobb-Douglas, CES, and Translog specifications estimated by OLS). Separate results given for eastern and western Germany. Establishment controls include log of capital (as proxied by replacement investment) and employment, the percentage of qualified employees and of sales exported, and dummies for profit sharing for employees, process innovation, use of apprentices, and coverage by a collective agreement (plus 15 sector dummies).	Works council presence is associated with sharply higher labor productivity of 25% (30%) for western (eastern) Germany. Disaggregations by manufacturing and service sectors largely confirm this basic result for eastern Germany; but for west German manufacturing industry the works council coefficient estimate is statistically insignificant. Profit sharing is positively associated with value-added in western Germany alone. But the works council-profit sharing interaction term is nowhere statistically significant. Collective bargaining coverage has a statistically significant (positive) coefficient for eastern Germany alone.
2. Schank, Schnabel, and Wagner (2004)	As above, 1993–2000. Unbalanced (n = 2,301) and balanced (n = 592) sample of west German establishments with 21–100 employees.	Log total sales	Fixed-effects estimation of a stochastic frontier production function. The comparison is between the technical efficiency estimates—and their 95% confidence intervals—of the median works council plant and its works council free counterpart.	There are no statistically significant differences in efficiency between establishments with and without work councils. Results are robust to outliers.

Continued

73

Table 6.1A Continued

Study	Data	Dependent Variable(s)	Methodology	Findings
3. Addison, Schank, Schnabel, and Wagner (2006)	As above, 1997–2000. Full sample comprises 11,464 observations and 5,684 establishments.	Log total sales.	OLS and fixed-effect estimates of a Translog production function supplemented with OLS estimates of a Cobb-Douglas production function in differences. For the production function estimates using pooled data, results are given for all industries and for manufacturing and services distinguishing by establishment size (all plants and plants with 21–100 employees) and each of the four cross-sections. The fixed-effects regressions were run separately for all industries, for smaller firms with 21–100 employees, for western and eastern Germany, and for manufacturing and services. The Cobb-Douglas function in differences was run for all plants and for the smaller firm subsample for Germany as a whole and for eastern and western Germany.	For the regressions using pooled data the all-firm works council "effect" on productivity was around 25 percent. For the subsample of plants with 21–100 employees, however, the coefficient estimates for the works council dummy fell sharply and were actually negative albeit statistically insignificant in the case of the manufacturing sector in western Germany. And for the repeated cross-sections they were statistically insignificant in three out of four years for the service sector. When controlling for time-invariant unobserved plant heterogeneity, the works council coefficient was statistically significant in just one case (out of six). Finally, there was no sign that sales in plants with works councils over the whole period grew either more quickly or more slowly than in their counterparts without councils over the whole period.

74

| 4. Addison, Bellmann, Schnabel, and Wagner (2004) | As above, 1996–2000. Initial sample of 1,544 establishments, all without works councils in 1996. | Changes in quits, sales per employee, employment, and profitability. | Nonparametric propensity score matching model. "Treated" group comprises all plants in which a works council was set up between 1996 and 1998. Matched plants derived from the 1,513 controls. | Mean values for the performance indicators in establishments that introduced works councils are not statistically different from those of comparator plants that remained works council free. Results are robust to outliers. |
| 5. Addison, Schank, Schnabel, and Wagner (2007) | As above, 1998–2003. Full sample of between 1,746 and 1,780 but plants changing works council status amounted to just 37 (14 formed, 23 dissolved). | Two investment measures: total investment and expansion investment divided by sales, averaged over 2000–2003. | Nonparametric (propensity score matching) analysis and parametric (OLS regression) analysis of investment across four types of establishments: those that never had a works council, those that did not have a works council at start of period but did at end of period, those that always had a works council, and those that had a works council at beginning of period but not at end of period. | Matching plant analysis revealed that neither works council formation nor dissolution (1998–2000) affected subsequent investment behavior vis-à-vis controls (those plants that never had a council and always had a council, respectively). Changes in works council status also statistically insignificant in investment functions estimated over all four types of plants. When investment functions estimated for separate samples of plants that never (always) had a works council to predict investment in plants that set up a works council (dissolved) a works council there was no indication that setting up a works council resulted in a statistically significant difference between actual and predicted investment while in those plants that abandoned a works council there was even some indication that investment was smaller than predicted. |

Continued

Table 6.1A Continued

Study	Data	Dependent Variable(s)	Methodology	Findings
6. Addison, Bellmann, and Kölling (2004)	As above, 1996–2000. Full sample of 3,693 establishments of which 243 closed.	Plant closings.	Probit estimates for the following samples: all plants; plants stratified by whether or not they are covered by collective agreements; plants stratified by size (less than or more than 50 employees); and plants stratified by both collective agreement coverage and size.	For the all-plant sample, works councils positively associated with plant closings. The works council effect is stronger in this regard for the uncovered sector and for smaller plants but the difference with their counterparts (in the uncovered sector and in larger plants, respectively) is not statistically significant. Only in the case of a separate sample of smaller plants is there any indication that collective bargaining coverage materially lowers the closure rate.
7. Addison and Teixeira (2006)	As above, 1993–2001. Sample size without (with) attritions is 143 (232) for the subsample of establishment with 21–100 employees and 600 (1,106) for the full sample of plants with ≥ 5 employees.	Employment growth is measured relative to average employment and also relative to base-year employment.	Conventional employment change equations estimated by OLS plus two specifications allowing for survival bias. The first treats plant closings as a 100% reduction in employment and is estimated by OLS. The second provides a selectivity-adjusted employment	Works councils are associated with a reduction in employment growth in the order of 2–3 percent a year. No strong evidence that this result is influenced by survival bias. Dynamic labor demand model confirms direction of works council influence but the point estimate is not statistically significant.

8. Jirjahn, (2008a)[b]	Employment growth.	Further, it provides no indication that works councils aggravate the already tortuous process of employment adjustment in Germany.
As above, 1993–2001. Sample size is 906 and for subsample that did not change their works council status it is 705.	change model estimated using maximum likelihood methods. Also separate estimation of a dynamic labor demand model using the GMM-SYS estimator. This model provides estimates of the impact of the works council on speed of employment adjustment as well as its effect on employment growth.	
	OLS regressions. Regressors include establishment size (entered linearly, in logs, and in quadratic form in separate specifications), short-time working, overtime working, Saturday work, legal form of the enterprise, technological status of capital equipment, shares of trainees and of low- and highly skilled workers, plus dummy variables (nine each) for economic sector and for the old federal states/city states.	Works councils are associated with lower employment growth where the size of establishment variable is entered linearly or log linearly. But the coefficient estimate for the works council dummy is statistically insignificant when employment size is entered in quadratic form. These results hold for both the full sample and for the main subsample, as well as for a different measure of employment growth (viz. difference in log employment between 2001 and 1993). In the case of plants with 21–100 employees, however, while negatively signed, the works council coefficient is statistically insignificant throughout, irrespective of the manner in which establishment size is measured.

Continued

Table 6.1A Continued

Study	Data	Dependent Variable(s)	Methodology	Findings
9. Boockmann and Hagen (2001)[c]	As above, 1993–1999.	Atypical work, namely, use of fixed-term contract workers (FTC), agency temporaries (AT), and freelancers (FL).	Random effects probit models of the likelihood of employing the three groups of atypical workers, thus controlling for unobserved firm-specific heterogeneity. Separate estimates according to whether the measure of output change is actual or expected sales. Other regressors in addition to dummies for works council presence and collective agreement coverage are (dummies for) seasonal fluctuations in demand, firm size, technology, and workforce problems stemming from maternity leave and sickness, and the shares of skilled and female workers.	Use of FTC workers is positively associated with works council presence. But neither AT work nor FL working is associated with works councils. The impact of collective agreement coverage is statistically insignificant throughout with the exception of a strongly negative association between sectoral agreements and the probability of employing FL workers (who are often covered by collective agreements).

[a] See also Frick (2002a, 2002b).
[b] See also Jirjahn (2008b).
[c] See also Bellmann (2003), Düll and Ellguth (1999), Hagen and Boockmann (2002).

disaggregation. For example, it vanishes for smaller manufacturing plants in western Germany with 21–100 employees. Moreover, once the authors control for time-invariant unobserved plant heterogeneity, they report much smaller coefficient estimates for the works council dummy that are (weakly) statistically significant only in one instance. It is therefore concluded that reports of a positive works council productivity effect have been much exaggerated.

In the row 4 productivity study, Addison, Bellmann, Schnabel, and Wagner (2004) formally exploit changes in works council status through time. Since this study focuses on recent changes in the law facilitating works council formation—the 2001 Works Constitution Act—its concern is with the introduction of works councils rather than with their introduction *and* dissolution (but see below). The authors' empirical strategy reflects their concern with the selection problem. They use a formal matching model to compare the (31) establishments that subsequently experienced the election of a works council with their closest counterparts from among the firmament of (1,513) plants that remained continuously free of works councils over the sample period. Again (the change in) productivity is proxied by the change in sales per employee rather than by value-added because the missing values problem alluded to earlier assumes critical importance given the small number of plants with new councils. The bottom line from this study is that there are no statistically significant differences between the treatment group and the controls in respect of productivity.

As can be seen, productivity is just one of four performance outcomes investigated in this study. Also examined are changes in the quit rate, changes in the profit situation, and changes in employment (on which more below). In no case, however, are the mean values of these performance indicators statistically different as between the treatment group and the controls. In short, the study is unable to reject the null that the introduction of a works council has no effect on any of the measures of establishment performance examined.

Attention shifts in row 5 to investment. Investment is a key but neglected indicator in the German literature.[4] A firm's investment in physical capital offers a classical vehicle for rent seeking on the part of labor. Works councils may in principle expropriate part of the quasirents that form part of the normal return to capital but that are vulnerable to capture once investment in specialized plant and equipment has been made. Knowing this, firms will respond by investing less. Such adverse effects on investment have been extensively reported for the United States (e.g., Hirsch, 1991). But of course this evidence pertains to unionism and as we have seen throughout this book works councils have typically been viewed in more favorable light, partly it has to be said by virtue of the limits placed on their ability to engage in rent seeking and not simply through (potentially) pro-productive routes such as encouraging workers to take a longer-term view of the enterprise and its prospects.

Here, as in the previous study, Addison, Schank, Schnabel, and Wagner (2007) use a matching approach, supplemented in this case with a parametric analysis. Unlike the study in row 4, however, this treatment examines works council dissolution as well as formation. But in both cases the focus is on within-plant changes rather than between-plant comparisons. Addison, Schank, Schnabel, and Wagner examine the impact of a regime shift (the setting up or the abandonment of a works council) between 1998 and 2000 on investment over the next three years. Plants that set up (dissolved) works councils between 1998 and 2000 are first matched with their twins that never (always) had a council, and mean values of the subsequent investment outcomes for the respective plant types compared. Second, investment functions are estimated across all four types of plants, and then separately for plants that never (always) had a works council to predict investment in plants that set up (dissolved) a works council. Neither the nonparametric nor the parametric exercises give any indication that works council formation (dissolution) had an unfavorable (favorable) impact on investment.[5]

The next three studies in table 6.1A deal with employment. The study by Addison, Bellmann, and Kölling (2004) in row 6 of the table provides the first analysis for Germany of the relation between works councils and plant closings. It reports statistically significant positive associations between works council presence and plant closings holding other things constant. This cet. par. result does not appear to be materially influenced by collective bargaining proper, with the possible exception of a small plant subsample, comprising establishments with less than 50 employees, where covered plants do appear to have lower closure rates. Although attributing causality to these results is fraught with difficulty given the nonrandom distribution of works councils and other unobserved heterogeneity, there is nonetheless the suggestion that estimates of the effects of works councils on more traditional performance outcomes should attempt to adjust for failure rates, that is, to control for possible survivor bias. In the event that works councils drive weaker firms out of business negative effects on performance might be understated and positive effects exaggerated—even if the welfare implications are more complicated where the entity speeds up a necessary process of adaptation to change.

It was reported earlier that employment growth in establishments setting up work councils for the first time does not differ significantly from that of their matched counterparts that never introduced a council. But the more conventional employment change study by Addison and Teixeira (2006) in row 7 of the table finds that employment growth is slowed in the presence of works councils. This finding echoes that reported in the Anglo-Saxon literature.[6] But the estimate of slowed employment growth of between 2 and 3 percent a year does not appear to be materially affected by selection. Works councils are associated with a lower probability of plant survival but the works council coefficient estimate in the selection equation is not statistically significant, at least for this sample period. In turn, the selectivity-adjusted impact of works councils on employment growth while greater in absolute value does not differ significantly from the unadjusted estimates. Moreover, in estimating a dynamic labor demand model using panel estimation techniques, the authors report that works councils do not add to the legendary inertia of the employment adjustment process in Germany. It is also the case that this longitudinal component of their analysis fails to confirm the negative effect on employment growth reported in the main body of their analysis, although the authors caution that the panel is likely too short to address the employment growth issue satisfactorily in a dynamic model of this type.

Using the same data set, the row 8 study by Jijahn (2008a) contends that negative works council employment "effects" are an artifact of the manner in which a key independent variable—establishment employment size—is measured. As do Addison and Teixeira (2006), he reports that the coefficient estimate for the works council dummy in the standard employment growth equation is both negative and well determined when establishment employment size is entered linearly (or in logarithmic form), but that it becomes insignificant when establishment size is a quadratic in employment. Indeed, as we have seen, in a separate analysis using data from the Hanover Firm Panel, 1994–1997, Jirjahn (2008b) goes so far as to claim that works councils increase employment. He obtains this result after allowing for the endogeneity of the works council entity. Specifically, he argues that works councils are formed to protect worker interests (characterized as quasi-rents) when the establishment is *in extremis* (or confronts "long-term financial pressure"). Jirjahn's selection equation uses all the same arguments as are used in the base OLS employment growth equation plus a variable identifying whether or not active owners are present in the establishment. Their presence is supposed to stimulate works council formation negatively but to have no direct employment effects. While his OLS estimates point to a works council coefficient estimate that is positive but insignificant, his ML (treatment effects) model suggest that works councils elevate employment growth by 7 percentage points per year (and by somewhat less than this in covered establishments). Now absence of a works council effect *is* an issue raised by the German research (cf. row 7 with rows 4 and 8 of table 6.1A) if not the Anglo-Saxon union literature where the evidence of negative association between the outcome indicator and the workplace representation entity is overwhelming (if not always easy to interpret). But to suggest that works councils increase employment is likely a step too far given the indirectness of the test, the nature of the exclusion restriction, the use of just three years of data, and above all the difficulty in modeling works council endogeneity in cross-section.

One reason for expecting works councils to influence employment is of course that they have extensive competence in this area. Consider, for example, the following powers earlier identified in chapter 2: the work council may submit proposals relating to the security and promotion of employment; in establishments with more than 500 employees it may request the drawing up of guidelines on the personal, technical, and social criteria to be applied in the selection of employees for recruitment, transfer, regrading, and dismissal; in establishments with more than 20 employees it has to be notified in advance by the employer of any recruitment, grading, and transfer and its consent obtained for the measures envisaged; it has also to be consulted on each and every dismissal, which is rendered null and void absent that approval; and in establishments with more than 20 employees the employer must notify it in full and good time of any proposed "alterations" (such as reductions in force, full or partial plant closures, and important changes in plant organization, purpose, or equipment), with the works council having the right to negotiate a social plan in compensation for these alterations. Not surprisingly, therefore, a number of studies have sought to examine the issue of how works councils might influence workplace flexibility.

The final study in row 9 of the table is representative of such analyses. Boockmann and Hagen (2001) focus on the use of flexible forms of employment or atypical work. Three types of atypical work are examined: fixed-term contracts, temporary agency work, and freelance work. Although the authors see the works council effect as secondary in importance to the role of other factors (such as temporary fluctuations in demand, protection of the core workforce, meeting temporary absences of regular employees, and changes in the law on dismissals), they accord works councils a potentially important role as well. Thus, it is hypothesized that competences such as those identified in the previous paragraph—together with codetermination in the area of overtime working—by increasing the procedural complexities and the costs of hiring and firing may indirectly be expected to lead to greater use of atypical workers. By the same token, it is also recognized that works councils (and collective bargaining) may directly militate against the use of atypical work.

Boockmann and Hagen estimate separate equations for each type of atypical work using a probit model that controls for unobserved heterogeneity. It is reported that works councils are associated with greater use of fixed-term contracts, consistent with the firing costs argument. But works councils seemingly have no effects on the use of temporary agency workers or freelancers. The former result is confirmed in a number of other studies also using the IAB Establishment Panel (e.g., Bellmann, 2003; Hagen and Boockmann, 2002; Düll and Ellguth, 1999), although findings with respect to the use of agency temps are mixed (see Bellmann, 2003, for a contrary finding).

The bottom line of the employment adjustment studies is that works councils do not seem to impact the speed of adjustment. Employers can presumably respond by adjusting along other margins such as the deployment of fixed term contract workers. Although these are higher cost options, the relative importance of the works council versus the law on dismissals is unclear in this respect. Further, some have argued that any reduction in external labor market flexibility where observed might be offset by increased internal flexibility (see Ellguth and Promberger, 2004). At issue is whether we can speak of a costless "regulation of flexibility" as these authors suggest.

Finally, returning to the first study in the table, Frick and Möller find that the presence of a works council has a negative and statistically significant effect on labor turnover in German establishments. However, this is by no means a universal finding from studies using the Establishment Panel (see, for example, the study in row 4 of the table) and even if it were we do not know whether turnover is too low or too high. Some hints are offered by the association between training and productivity reported in the next subsection.

6.3.2 Employee Involvement, High Performance Work Practices, and Works Councils

As was seen in the previous chapter,[7] discussion of the effects of worker representation in Germany has become linked with those of innovative work practices. This is hardly surprising since the arguments favoring works councils and employee involvement/high performance work practices (EI/HPWPs) are closely linked. Table 6.1B provides a selective review of the most important recent studies using the IAB Establishment Panel. The themes of this literature include incentivization issues, complementarities, and training. Taken in the round, the studies point to circumstances in which works councils may be associated with favorable productivity outcomes even if the links between worker representation and EI/HPWPs are not yet transparent.[8]

All the studies in the table follow a common methodology suggested by Black and Lynch (2001) in estimating production functions for a large nationally representative sample of U.S. manufacturing firms with panel data for 1987–1993. Black and Lynch use a two-stage procedure that involves first estimating a fixed, time-invariant firm effect for each establishment using data for the time-varying factors—namely, capital, labor, and raw materials—and then regress these fixed effects (or firm-level efficiency parameters) on all the time-invariant and near-time invariant factors (that in their case include EI/HPWPs, technology, and worker characteristics).[9] In this second step, the endogeneity of the HPWPs can also be allowed for. It follows that the modern German literature places especial emphasis on unobserved plant heterogeneity and selection issues.

The analysis by Wolf and Zwick (2002, 2008) in row 1 of the table provides the template for all the studies. Wolf and Zwick focus on the productivity of HPWPs. They identify six such practices, which are reduced to two independent factors—termed "organizational changes" (including the delegation of authority and decisions to lower levels of the hierarchy, participatory practices such as teamwork, and workgroups with and independent budget) and "incentives" (e.g., profit sharing)—using principal components analysis. The authors fit an augmented Cobb-Douglas production function to IAB cross-section data for 1999, including a selectivity-adjusted specification. They also fit a Cobb-Douglas function to data for 1996–1999 using panel estimation methods, and derive a fixed time-invariant establishment-specific effect for each plant after Black and Lynch, which values are then regressed on the time-invariant covariates—including organizational changes and

Table 6.1B The Economic Impact of Innovative Work Practices and Works Councils on Performance—Phase 3 Studies

Study	Data	Methodology	EI/HPWP Measure	Works Council Variable	Findings
1. Wolf and Zwick (2002, 2008)	IAB Establishment Panel, for a 1999 cross-section and a 1996–1999 panel.	Cobb-Douglas production function, with capital approximated by replacement investments. Dependent variable: value-added and average value-added. Cross-section estimates with and without correction for endogeneity of HPWPs. For the panel, the estimation follows the Black-Lynch (2000, 2004) two-step procedure (see text), with the second stage also controlling for the endogeneity of HPWPs.	Six HPWPs: shifting of responsibilities to lower level in hierarchy; teamwork; work groups with independent budgets; employee share ownership; profit sharing; training to support organizational change; and incentive training. These HPWPs are aggregated into two independent factors ("organizational change" and "incentives") using principal components factor analysis and are subsequently instrumented using five exclusion restrictions.	Works council presence—exogenous.	In cross-section, the positive effect of "incentives" (share ownership, profit sharing, supportive training, and incentive training) results from their being introduced by firms when they are prospering. Interaction effects between organizational changes and incentives bundles are negative but statistically insignificant in cross-section after controlling for selection. In the panel (second-step) estimates and after correcting for selection, "organizational changes" (shifting responsibilities, teamwork, and independent work groups) have a significantly positive effect on productivity. Such changes are introduced to deal with structural problems, so-called structural productivity gaps. The separate works council effect is not robust in cross-section, but in panel estimates work council presence has significantly positive impact on the establishment-specific fixed effect.

Continued

Table 6.1B Continued

Study	Data	Methodology	EI/HPWP Measure	Works Council Variable	Findings
2. Zwick (2004)	IAB Establishment Panel, 1997–2000.	Cobb-Douglas production analysis function, with capital constructed using the perpetual inventory method after Black and Lynch (2001). Dependent variable: value-added and average value-added. In other words, the same two-step procedure used by Wolf and Zwick (2002, 2008) with GMM (GMM-SYS) estimator to give improved precision over the within estimator in first step.	"Participative work forms" based on delegation of responsibility and decision making to lower levels in the hierarchy, teamwork, and work groups with independent budgets. These three measures are aggregated to form a single participation variable set equal to one if at least one of the three measures had been introduced in 1996 or 1997. (For some specifications, the author also constructs an independent "participation factor" based on principal component factor analysis of the three measures.) Participation is endogenized using instrumental variable regressions. The external	Works council presence, and estimated works council presence in a switching regression model. The identifying variable is the existence of profit sharing or employee share ownership in 1998.	After accounting for the endogeneity of participative work forms, the productivity effect of such practices is 28 percent, considerably higher than the 9 percent value obtained in the OLS estimates. In the switching regression (the instrumented value for) participation is only (marginally) statistically significant in the sample of works council firms. Selection into works council status is well determined in both equations.

| 3. Zwick (2005) | IAB Establishment Panel. Cross-sections for 1997, 1998, and 1999, and panel data for 1997–2001. | Cobb-Douglas production function approach. Dependent variable: value-added, average value-added. Cross-section estimates of effect of continuous vocational training in 1997 on labor productivity levels in 1998 and 1999. Selection into training status handled through a single correction term based on a probit estimate of whether the firm offers training of any sort. (The identifying variables comprise three arguments reflecting expected skill gaps and two arguments expressing the reactions of the personnel instruments are two variables capturing expected skill gaps and two types of training (job rotation ands self-induced training) that are expected to increase in frequency in the following two years. | Seven training types: formal external training, formal internal training, training on the job, seminars and talks, job rotation, self-induced learning, and quality circles. Model also includes employee participation (shifting of responsibilities to lower level in hierarchy), teamwork, work groups with independent budgets, and incentive payments (profit related pay or employee share ownership). | Works council presence—exogenous. | In cross-section, (lagged) effects of formal external training courses on productivity are positive and statistically significant throughout. But training on-the-job is negatively associated with productivity. The selection term is positive suggesting establishments with a "productivity disadvantage" train more. Employee participation and incentive payment coefficient estimates are nowhere significant. The panel estimates indicate that formal external courses and quality circles have a positive and statistically significant association with productivity, whereas the relation with training on the job is again negative and well determined. After selection is accounted for, the coefficient estimate for formal external training courses increases in magnitude. Coefficient estimate for the works council dummy is positive and statistically |

Continued

Table 6.1B Continued

Study	Data	Methodology	EI/HPWP Measure	Works Council Variable	Findings
		department to these shortages.) Fixed-effects panel estimation using two-step procedure as in row 2 study, also with and without selectivity correction.			significant in the probit estimates and the second-step regression estimates.
4. Zwick (2006)	IAB Establishment Panel, 1997 and panel data for 1998–2001.	Cobb-Douglas production function approach. Dependent variable: average (fixed) productivity, using two-step procedure as above. OLS and panel OLS with instrumental variable estimation.	Training intensity as measured by the number of employees trained in the first half of 1997 divided by the number of employees on the books as of June 1997. Intensity is endogenized using instrumental variable regressions. Model also includes employee participation (as defined in row 3), teamwork, work groups with independent budgets, stringent formal hiring rules, and incentive payments (as defined in row 3).	Works council presence —exogenous.	Training intensity explained by demand factors, existence of apprenticeship training, and collective bargaining coverage but not works councils. Coefficient for predicted (but not actual) training intensity is positive and well determined. Again the suggestion is that greater training intensity occurs in times of productivity disadvantage. While individual HPWP coefficients are individually statistically insignificant they are jointly significant.

incentives—again allowing for selection. But note that the data set only enables the authors to identify whether or not the innovative practices were present at a point in time, not when they had been introduced.

As shown in table 6.1B, both selection and accounting for structural differences matter. The positive effect on productivity of incentive mechanisms, observed in both cross-section and in the panel, seem to result from such schemes being introduced in times of plenty, when firms are doing well. That is, after correction for the endogeneity of such measures, the variable is no longer statistically significant. For their part, the effect of organizational changes is statistically insignificant in cross-section, with and without correction for selection. However, the coefficient estimate is both positive and well determined in the panel estimates, and after controlling for selection strengthens somewhat. The main message of this study, therefore, is that firms that introduce organizational changes seemingly have unobserved time-invariant characteristics that decrease their productivity. Expressed differently, participatory work practices (alone) raise productivity.

The role of the work council is secondary in Wolf and Zwick. The measured effect of the entity is positive and statistically significant in the second-step fixed effects estimation but clearly interpretation is difficult where the production functions differ by works council status and if there is a correlation between the presence of a works council and unobserved time-invariant plant level characteristics or the establishment fixed effect.

In the next study (row 2 of the table) the role of the works council shares equal billing with innovative work practices. Here, Zwick (2004) considers just those practices found to be statistically significant in Wolf and Zwick—namely, organizational changes, now termed "participation"—and considers their impact on productivity over the same interval, albeit using a different panel estimator for the (first-stage) production function and now controlling for the endogeneity of works council presence (as well as that of the participation variable). Other differences reside in the measurement of capital and the construction of the participation measure.

Zwick's second-step regression results for a specification in which works councils are assumed exogenous indicates that the innovative work practice(s) is positive and well determined, elevating productivity by 25 percent. However, accounting for the nonrandom distribution of works councils in an endogenous switching regression model shows that the pro-productive effect of participatory work practices (or one such practice) only obtains in works council firms. Although the story is similar to that told by Wolf and Zwick—in the sense that innovatory practices are conceived to rectify productivity gaps—the main result is distinct: innovations only bear fruit in works council regimes. (A similar result for two of the three elements in Zwick's participation dummy is also found in a study by Hübler and Jirjahn [2002] not reported in the table). Unfortunately, the coefficient estimate for the participation variable in works council plants is only statistically significant at the 0.10 level.

One of the routes through which works councils and all voice institutions are supposed to influence productivity is by encouraging investments by the firm in training. Although as we have seen, the German literature has dwelt at some length on the labor turnover issue (see also below), there has been little direct analysis of further training until comparatively recently. The last two studies in the table examine this issue. The study by Zwick (2005) in row 3 examines the determinants of training and the impact of seven types of training on labor productivity. As in the two preceding studies, the basic framework is again a mix of cross-section and two-stage panel estimation (using the GMM-SYS estimator in the first step) with endogenous training. In addition to detailed establishment controls, the equations include three other innovative work practices. These are identical to those previously grouped under "participation" in the row 2 study, namely, a shifting of responsibilities to lower levels in the hierarchy, the presence of teamwork and self-directed groups, and work groups/units with their own costs and results accounting. Incentive pay is also used as a regressor. All these practices are now treated as exogenous, as is works council presence.

In cross-section, Zwick (2005) finds that lagged formal external training consistently records a positive association with productivity while training-on-the-job mostly evinces a negative association. The selection correction term is positive. And the coefficient estimate for the former variable increases sharply with correction for selection.[10] The suggestion is, then, that such training tends to be offered during "times of productivity disadvantage." The coefficient estimates for the participation and incentive regressors are statistically insignificant throughout.

The effect of the panel estimation is also to increase the measured impact of all types of training. As before, the sign of the selection correction term is positive. Both formal external training and quality circles are associated with higher average productivity of 28 percent and 17 percent, respectively. Also as before, the other training types do not have any (longer-term) productivity impact and the same obtains for participation and incentives. Finally, for their part works councils appear to be positively associated with training incidence *and* with average productivity. The latter result holds for both the cross-sectional and panel analyses, although we note that works council endogeneity is not modeled.

The final study in row 4 of the table considers the *intensity* (strictly, coverage) of training. Here, Zwick (2006) reports that the intensity of training is a source of improved productivity once selectivity bias is taken into account. Zwick corrects for selectivity using a similar (but reduced) set of identifying restrictions as in Zwick (2004). He finds that a one percentage point increase in training intensity (measured over the first six months of 1997) is associated with a 0.76 percentage point increase in average establishment productivity over 1998–2001. The individual performance of the other HPWPs is unimpressive, although they are jointly statistically significant. Further, interaction terms between training and these practices were statistically insignificant throughout. For its part, works council presence reemerges as pro-productive.

As before, it is argued that failure to account for selectivity reduces the measured productivity impact of training. Increased training intensity is seen as a remedial strategy. As Zwick (2006, p. 42) concludes, "one motivation of establishments to increase training intensity is an attempt to regain competitiveness and to close qualification gaps because training is a suitable means to reduce these gaps with respect to competitors."

German work on HPWPs in some sense mirrors that in the United States (e.g., Ichniowski and Shaw, 1996; Ichniowski, Kochan, Levine, and Strauss, 1996; Cappelli and Neumark, 2001). Thus, there is no agreement on the role of individual practices—the disputation over profit sharing is perhaps the main case in point—and on complementarities between them. In addressing the issue of complementarities, Wolf and Zwick (2002, 2008) include a specification in their first set of cross-section estimates that contains an interaction term between the two bundles of personnel measures, namely, "organizational change" and "incentives." The interaction term is significantly negative, suggesting that in combination both sets of measures decrease productivity. In a separate specification, they enter each of the components of the two bundles individually and look for complementarities. Although most of the measures have a positive impact on productivity this is not true of teamwork whose coefficient estimate is negative and statistically significant. And there are few signs of complementarities between the individual measures. Just one interaction term is positive and significant (the delegation of authority to lower levels in the organization and teamwork) while yet others are negative and statistically insignificant (e.g., delegation and training induced by organizational measures). Having corrected for the endogeneity of the HPWPs, however, the authors report that the interaction term between the two bundles while negative is no longer statistically significant, leading them to conclude that when both sets of practices are *jointly* introduced it is at times of productivity disadvantage.

The only other study in the table to examine potential complementarities is Zwick (2006) in row 4. In unreported estimates, he notes the results of interacting training intensity with investments in ICT and with five personnel management methods (shifting of responsibilities to lower ranks, teamwork, units with their own cost and results accounting, stringent hiring rules, and incentive payments). No significant interaction terms could be identified.

The often insignificant results for HPWPs are not restricted to the German literature and may reflect the lack of truly longitudinal data on the various practices and inadequate information on coverage as much as they do factors such as bad synchronization and collinearities in the case of complementarities. But the most important result of the German literature is that practices that appear to have no positive value emerge on closer inspection to be productive while yet others that are seemingly productive are seen after controlling for their endogeneity to have no effect on performance. This is the truly distinctive contribution—namely, instrumenting two bundles of personnel measures—while paying equally close attention to the issue of unobserved plant heterogeneity.

A final issue is whether works councils and HPWPs are substitutes or complements. The earlier literature provided examples of each. A substitute relation was suggested by the finding of a negative association between teamworking and works council presence (Addison, Schabel, and Wagner, 1997) and the greater frequency of HPWPs in the absence of works councils (or, in their presence, where works councils are antagonistic). A complementary relation was suggested by the finding of a positive association between works councils and group incentives (subject to disagreement about the impact of the latter on performance) and between works councils and training (Gerlach and Jirjahn, 2001). Evidence from the IAB Establishment Panel is also mixed both as regards the role of the entity as a determinant of employee involvement/high performance work practices and the relation between works councils and the labor productivity effect of those practices. We have cited the result from Zwick (2004) that participative work forms are only pro-productive in works council regimes. We did not give chapter and verse on another German study by Hübler and Jirjahn (2002) that reports a negative interaction effect between works councils and the labor productivity effect stemming from a reduction in hierarchies (but a positive interaction effect of works councils and the introduction of teams on productivity). In sum, the evidence on the covariation of works councils and employee involvement is mixed and partly contradictory (Zwick, 2004, p. 719). This is not surprising given the lingering imprecision of the Anglo-Saxon literature, underscored by the inertia in works council presence. But despite these and other concerns the German literature suggests that works councils and innovative practices can have favorable effects on productivity that may on occasion be reinforcing. We are just beginning to investigate the latter links and these may be rather complex with direct and indirect links between works councils and EI/HPWPs pulling in different directions.[11] A major lacuna remains the issue of cost: we have no information on the costs of those innovative work practices that are measured as pro-productive.

6.3.3 Works Councils and Wages

Prior to the publication of the IAB Establishment Panel (and the LIAB in particular) study of the effect of works councils on wages was limited. This neglect was largely data driven. The fact that some of the best of the early research failed to detect any work council impact on wages—possibly in association with section 77 (c) of the Works Constitution Act—may also have played a role, leading researchers to pursue other questions (see chapters 4 and 5) and other potential sources of inefficiency such as slowed decision making and bloated payrolls. Even today research in this area is a still comparatively sparse but wage research is moving toward center stage and may well come to dominate modern investigation of works council impact in the future. Collective bargaining proper will of course figure no less centrally than works councils in this endeavor.

We proceed to trace the thrust of contemporary research in this area. But since we have somewhat neglected the wage literature up to this point because of its minor place in the evolving research on works council impact, it is now time briefly to take stock as it were of the pre-IAB findings. The starting point is of course FitzRoy and Kraft's (1985) analysis of 60 firms in the metal working industry, using pooled data for 1977 and 1979. The main emphasis of this study is upon profitability, but wages are also examined in the authors' system of simultaneous equations (see table 4.1, row 1). FitzRoy and Kraft fail to detect any positive effect of works councils on wages. They do report that *union density* has a positive and statistically significant effect on wages, but even here the link is indirect. The mechanism is as follows. Hard-driving managers are held to elicit higher productivity from their workers and are rewarded with higher salaries and profits. The pressure exerted by management causes workers to join unions and unionized workers get higher wages even if this is only partial compensation for their greater effort. In other words, the line of causation is from performance to workplace density as workers react defensively to the higher demands made of them by management.

But the evidence from the early, Phase 1 studies is far from uniform. Thus, for example, in an analysis of 50 industrial firms in 1990/1991, Addison, Kraft, and Wagner (1993) obtain a significantly positive coefficient estimate for the works council dummy in conventional OLS and least median of squares/reweighted least squares wage regressions.

More recent Phase 2 studies using larger datasets range a little wider. In an analysis of the first wave of the Hanover Firm Panel (*Hannoveraner Firmenpanel*) covering manufacturing establishments in Lower Saxony, Addison, Schnabel, and Wagner (2001) report in OLS wage regressions that wages are approximately 15–18.5 percent higher in works council regimes (see also Meyer, 1995b). The authors also investigate the gap between the wage fixed at industry/regional level and that paid at the establishment, using management-reported estimates of the percentage wage gap (*übertarifliche Entlohnung*).[12] The authors' Tobit estimates fail to indicate any influence of works councils on the wage gap for either blue-collar or white-collar employees. However, in exploiting a question in the panel inquiring of managers whether or not the works council was jointly involved in determining the wage gap, Addison, Schnabel, and Wagner report that the gap is higher where the works council is involved in wage determination.

As we have seen in chapter 5, further differentiation is offered by the introduction of collective bargaining arguments proper and the extension of the wage argument. Using two waves of the Hanover Firm Panel, Hübler and Jirjahn (2003) offer a test of the Freeman-Lazear (1995) argument model that, where a council is embedded in an external collective bargaining framework, councils and local management are likely to focus on maximizing the joint surplus. In contrast, where there is no collective agreement (external to the firm), there is said to be little to constrain rent-seeking councils.[13]

Interestingly, Hübler and Jirjahn report no evidence of an independent effect of collective bargaining on wages, the result of which they justify on the grounds that the outcome of collective agreements is usually extended to the overwhelming number of employees in an industry (but see below). However, their main results pertain to works councils, which were found to have a consistently positive effect on wages only in the uncovered sample. (The well-defined productivity effect of covered works councils was discussed in chapter 5.)

Somewhat different wage results are reported by Jirjahn (2003), using the same data set but not on this occasion controlling for works council endogeneity. His OLS estimates point to a works council wage premium in *both* sectors. That said, the measured works council effect is higher in uncovered than covered establishments (the works council mark-up is 19 percent and 9 percent, respectively). But in an update of Hübler and Jirjahn's wage analysis using IAB data (see below) for the Lower Saxony subsample, Gerlach and Meyer (2007) do report a straightforward reversal of the Hübler-Jirjahn estimates; that is, the impact of works councils on wages is stronger in establishments covered by a collective agreement and weaker for uncovered establishments.[14]

Modern Phase 3 studies typically examine the effects of both institutions upon wages. But those that examine the impact on wages of collective bargaining alone point to a positive effect of coverage. Thus, for example, using the LIAB for 1996, Kölling, Schnabel, and Wagner (2005) find that collective bargaining at sectoral level raises wages, at least for the least-skilled workers. Another study by Stephan and Gerlach (2005), using linked employer-employee data from the German Structure of Earnings Survey for the Lower Saxony subsample, points to a positive premium for collective bargaining coverage. Specifically, over successive cross-sections of the data they report evidence of a rising wage premium for the average covered worker: 4 percent in 1991, through 9 percent in 1995, to 12 percent in 2001.[15]

The latest linked employer-employee studies examine both collective bargaining coverage and works council presence. Using LIAB data for the mining and manufacturing sector, 1995–2001, Gürtzgen (2009) investigates the manner in which wages respond to rents (defined as value-added minus the opportunity cost of labor). She reports that rent sharing is unrelated to collective bargaining coverage once one accounts for unobserved individual and plant heterogeneity *and* the endogeneity of rents. These findings are consistent with those of Hübler and Jirjahn (2003), but the explanation is more specific: unions favor a compressed intraindustry wage structure and suppress the responsiveness of wages to firm-specific profitability considerations.

Gürtzgen further reports a well-determined positive association between works councils and rent sharing in pooled OLS estimates. Works council presence increases wages by 11–15 percent. Although this effect falls to between 2 and 3 percent after controlling for unobserved individual and plant heterogeneity, it is still statistically significant and, further, survives the application of dynamic panel estimators.[16] Finally, Gürtzgen also provides results for specific groups of workers. Her fixed-effect estimates suggest that collective bargaining at sectoral level reduces the responsiveness of wages to establishment-specific profitability conditions in respect of males and females and by skill group. The works council effect on wages is positive for males, blue-collar workers, and medium- and high-skilled workers.

In a companion analysis, Gürtzgen (2006) estimates wage change models for individuals (and establishments) that change their collective bargaining status, using LIAB data for 1995–2002, and confirms her earlier result that centralized bargaining has modest effects, now increasing wages by 2 percent on average. Her simple pooled regression estimates point to positive cet. par. effects of sectoral collective bargaining of 8.1 percent (6.8 percent) in western (eastern) Germany. The interaction term between works councils and sectoral collective bargaining is positive and statistically significant, further elevating wages by some 5.6 (13.7) percent. However, other interaction terms indicate that collective bargaining at sectoral level reduces the returns to skill and gender, consistent with a narrowing of wage differentials (see also Heinze and Wolf, 2006). Allowing for the nonrandom selection of workers and firms into collective bargaining using a spell-differenced specification yields only a very modest sectoral collective bargaining differential of 2.3 percent (for western Germany alone) and few signs that collective bargaining now has any influence on the returns to worker characteristics. As far as works councils are concerned, wages are modestly higher (1.6 percent) where the plant is covered by a sectoral collective bargaining agreement (again for western Germany alone). Finally, Gürtzgen also examines whether switching contract status might hinge on time-specific as opposed to time-invariant unobservables. Her trend-adjusted difference-in-differences estimation strategy suggests that the 2.3 percent collective bargaining mark-up might now be an underestimate.

Finally, Addison, Teixeira, and Kraft (2009) examine the effect of works councils on wages using matched employer-employee data from the LIAB for 2001. They also take collective bargaining explicitly into account. On average, they report that works councils are associated with higher earnings even after accounting for establishment and worker heterogeneity. At this level, the works council premium exceeds the collective bargaining mark-up and is higher in the presence of collective bargaining once worker selection into plants with works councils and collective agreements is accounted for. Indeed, a works council premium is found for most groups with the principal exception of plants with 21–100 employees where a premium only obtains in covered establishments. But works councils also benefit some groups more than others. Women are a perhaps the most obvious beneficiary, a result that is amplified in covered works council establishments. If works councils are associated with any narrowing of the wage distribution this phenomenon emerges only in conjunction with collective bargaining.

The very latest treatments of *collective bargaining* of which we are aware seek to differentiate between union power, as measured by (predicted) union density, and individual and establishment collective bargaining coverage (sectoral and firm collective agreements). The upshot of these investigations by Fitzenberger, Kohn, and Lembcke (2006, 2008) using the German Structure of Earnings Survey for 2001 is not altogether clear-cut, partly because of the new element of individual bargaining coverage in covered firms (since not all employees are covered). But the main results of the authors' least squares wage level regressions are as follows. First, firms that follow a collective contract pay higher wages on average; specifically, the greater the share of workers in a firm covered by a collective contract, the higher is the wage. Second, individuals subject to a collective contract earn less, other things being equal—such that the net effect for a covered employee in a firm with full coverage is actually negative. Third, the interaction effect on individual coverage and firm coverage is negative so that on average a covered individual earns less than his/her uncovered counterpart in the same firm. That said, the effect of firm coverage is positive for both types of individual, it being more positive for uncovered individuals. Fourth, an increase in union density lowers wages. Allowing for interaction effects between union density and individual coverage serves to either reduce or negate the negative effect of being a covered individual in a covered firm.

Finally, quantile regressions add three additional main results. First, collective agreements have a similar effect on wages along the wage distribution (i.e., in raising wages). Second, coverage at the individual level reduces wage inequality, as its negative effects are higher in absolute terms at higher reaches of the distribution. Third, on balance union density reduces dispersion but its negative effects throughout the distribution (i.e., on uncovered workers, too) are also consistent with spillover effects. In capturing several dimensions of union influence on the structure of wages these are interesting results. But note there is no separate investigation of works council impact (the data set does not contain a works council question) and unlike Gürtzgen (and Addison, Terixeira, and Zwick [2009]) each union variable is considered exogenous.

The implications of the wage literature review are threefold. First and foremost, despite section 77 (3) of the Works Constitution Act, works councils may be expected to have some independent (positive) influence on wage levels, even if the manner of that influence along the skills continuum and the wage distribution is not transparent. Second, although the influence of collective bargaining proper is also clouded, there is nonetheless the suggestion that the wage effects of works councils are influenced by collective bargaining coverage. Third, and relatedly, it is inappropriate to treat the institutions of industrial relations as exogenous, notwithstanding the difficulty of accounting for their endogeneity.

6.4 Conclusions

Works council research in Germany has come of age. The issue of large data sets has been central to this development. We know much more than before about works council effects on firm performance and wage, including a sharper understanding of the limits/boundaries of our knowledge. And there is evidence of a learning experience on the part of researchers.

Interestingly, German research on works councils follows a very different history from the literature on workplace unions and firm performance in the United States although both approaches seem to end up telling much the same story about *productivity*. For its part the German literature has gone from rather pessimistic projections of works council impact on labor productivity through frankly Pollyanna-ish estimates toward a recognition that the effects are likely to be small on net and perhaps as likely to be positive as negative. The U.S. research began with pro-productivity effects in the order of 30 percent—much like those reported in early cross-sections using the IAB Establishment panel—and has gradually scaled back the estimates, ultimately converging on the same conclusion of small effects on average. So in both countries the trail returns to the factors producing shifts around what is likely to be a small effect on average. Factors flagged in the German case include establishment size, collective bargaining coverage, and innovative work practices. And for the future analysts may be able to exploit a new question in the Establishment Panel inquiring into the degree of cooperativeness of the works council, the limitation being that the question has thus far been restricted to the 2006 wave.

Analysts trying to determine the effects of German workplace representation have had to struggle with a wider set of difficulties than U.S. researchers studying unions. This is because of institutional inertia—very few works councils are set up or dissolved over the time intervals dictated by our samples—missing observations, and irregular survey questions. Nevertheless, a determined effort has been made to attempt to account for their nonrandom distribution over firms as a result of both observables and unobservables. Thus, the approaches used to deal with the problem of selectivity include instrumental variables estimation, selection models, the difference-in-differences estimator, and nonparametric matching methods. And from the latter attempts have come some of the more restrained estimates of works council impact on firm performance.

We feel most at home with the basic productivity findings. Equally modest works council effects probably obtain with respect to investments in physical capital (if correct this interpretation stands in sharp contrast with what has been reported in the U.S. *union* literature, but it would at least be consistent with other European research in this area). More controversial is works council impact on employment. There is some indication that works councils are associated with a higher rate of plant closings. However, if British evidence on unions and plant closings is anything to go by, interpretation of this result is clouded and its stability is in doubt. That said, a good case can be made that all other performance relationships should be checked for possible survival bias.

There is real controversy over the result that works councils slow employment growth, even if no study using the IAB Establishment Panel actually records higher employment growth in work council establishments. The association with labor turnover is also clouded for a number of reasons. Cross-section estimates always indicate lower quits in works council regimes, but allowing for works council endogeneity can overturn this result. And even if quits were unequivocally lower in the presence of works councils, this reduction could be excessive. Here the issue is one of the productivity of reduced turnover. Although we know of no attempt to run augmented production functions—that sequentially include a works council dummy and then a turnover (or tenure) variable, anticipating a reduction in the former coefficient estimate—we have discussed training studies that perhaps have a more direct bearing on the issue.

No less important an issue is the effect of works councils on employment adjustment. Longer panels are required to answer this question but the evidence we have uncovered thus far is that works councils do not seemingly aggravate the process of employment adjustment in Germany. But for the future a sharper distinction has to be made than heretofore between labor law (the law on dismissals protection) and the role of works councils. And so this is another question that we need to know more about.

German work on the effect of employee involvement/high performance practices as with similar studies in other countries is informative in permitting us to go behind the veil of collective voice. But also as in other countries German research has focused more on the effect of the practices themselves than their interaction with workplace representation. Accordingly, the main message of such studies may be that they identify aspects of the synthetic workplace, suggesting ways in which works councils may raise productivity. Perhaps the most interesting result uncovered in the studies examined here is that practices that appear to have no association with productivity or even a negative association may emerge on closer inspection (i.e., after allowing for their endogeneity) to be strongly pro-productive, and conversely. Further, we reported on one study in which participative mechanisms had a payoff solely in works council regimes. The problem here of course is that we cannot discount the possibility that the unobserved characteristic of good management lies at the heart of the observed relationship. Nevertheless, here is a result that at face value "explains" potentially large works councils "effects" on productivity. We also cited other research in this area pointing to the productivity of (some types of) training, and evidence of more training in works council regimes. This evidence is of course consistent with works councils reducing turnover and incentivizing employers to provide greater training. It may also be consistent with notions of contract enforcement. The argument has usually been made in respect of unions. Thus, Dustmann and Schönberg (2004) argue that the unavailability/infeasibility of long-term wage agreements means that training will be underprovided in regular markets and that unions move (apprenticeship) training closer to the social optimum by guaranteeing trained workers at least the union wage in the future.[17]

But there is also some evidence on substitutability between works councils and high performance management practices and so more work is needed in this area, not least because of the continuing allegations of a "codetermination-free" zone. Relatedly, perhaps the most important challenge to works councils is raised by work being undertaken on bodies analogous to works councils, namely, those entities defined in the IAB Establishment Panel as "other company-specific forms of staff representation." But research using this question, which was first asked in the 2003 wave of the Establishment Panel, is still sparse. This may reflect changes that have been made to the question. To date, research exploiting the question has focused on personnel issues alone, suggesting beneficial effects of the entities on labor turnover and training (see Ellguth, 2005, 2006). Further investigation of the role of these bodies is urgently required. Subject to a caveat regarding their joint presence with works councils, what implications do these bodies have for worker involvement in their companies and for their formal counterpart, the works council? And what impact do they have on productivity, profitability, investment, wages, and employment growth?

If it is thought that Phase 3 research with its focus on productivity has ranged more narrowly than heretofore, this is emphatically not the case for wages. German work on collective bargaining has also come of age with some impressive studies using linked employer-employee data. Here works councils have necessarily assumed secondary billing to collective bargaining proper. The importance of this literature for works councils is that it has allowed further scrutiny of the notion that where works councils are embedded in the dual system they will be more responsible and be less concerned with questions of distribution than with issues of production. A preliminary conclusion from the wage literature in this regard is that the Freeman-Lazear model has not fared too well. That is to say, although there are some contrary tendencies, there are clear signs in the wage literature that the impact of works councils on wages is stronger for firms covered by a collective agreement and weaker for works councils that are not covered by collective bargaining. (This result is stronger in smaller establishments, where there is no real indication of a works council mark-up.) That is perhaps the central result. A secondary result is that works councils benefit female workers in particular and more generally are associated with a narrowing of differentials *in conjunction with collective bargaining.* The results for collective bargaining coverage alone point to a positive wage premium and narrowed distribution, both of which are reduced > after the selection of firms (and workers) into collective agreements is taken into account. But there remain difficulties with the main identification strategy that is based on firms that switch their union status through time and workers who stay with the firm. In particular, it is unclear where the transitions come from: why do firms leave/join the employer association/switch union status?

There is also a suggestion in studies that do not take account of contract endogeneity that higher union density reinforces the effects of coverage. And in a link-up with the EI/HPWPs literature, the most recent wage research also indicates that innovative management practices might also reduce gender differences within plants. Interesting as these results are, the more pressing need is to better integrate the institutions of the dual system, clarifying the themes of worker selection into works councils and collective agreements and firm selection into firm level and sectoral level collective bargaining.

CHAPTER 7

Codetermination at the Enterprise Level

7.1 Introduction

Up to this point we have examined the effects of *betriebliche Mitbestimmung*, namely, the consequences for firm performance of worker representation in works councils at establishment or plant level. Now we turn to consider the impact of *Unternehmensmitbestimmung*, or worker representation on company boards. Inevitably this more aggregative consideration will compound the effects of codetermination at plant level. Since to all intents and purposes firms with worker directors will have works councils, there has been no attempt to separate out the effects of each. This should be borne in mind in what follows.

The institutional framework of board representation needs to be recalled at the outset. There are three different supervisory board regimes: full-parity codetermination for the coal and steel industries under the 1951 Codetermination Act; almost-equal or quasi-parity representation under the Codetermination Act of 1976 for corporations having more than 2,000 employees but where the chairman of the board, elected by the shareholders, has the casting vote in the event of a tie; and one-third board representation in companies with between 500 and 2000 employees under the Works Constitution Act of 1952. It will also be recalled from chapter 2 that the one-third board representation option has historically been viewed in Germany as an absence of codetermination (e.g., *Kommission Mitbestimmung*, 1998). But, as we shall see in chapter 8, use of the one-third rule as a default has been recently been revived by employers.

We also referred to the employer resistance occasioned by the 1976 Codetermination Act that extended (quasi-) parity codetermination.[1] Thus, we noted that 9 corporations and 29 employers associations challenged the 1976 Act on constitutional grounds, as infringing the property rights of shareholders. The Federal Constitutional Court in its decision of March 1, 1979, upheld the constitutionality of the law, arguing that shareholder rights were protected because the supervisory board chairman still had the casting vote, while noting that the private property rights enshrined in the constitution had also to serve *public* welfare as might obtain from heightened industrial peace and thence improved economic performance.[2] And, as we shall see, companies (and unions) have engaged courts at all levels on codetermination issues. Relatedly, it has been argued that employers also responded to the 1976 Act by scaling down the (employment) size of their operations and by divestiture. More tangibly, such actions in the case of the 1951 Act led to tightening up of *Montanmitbestimmung* in the form of amendments to the legislation in 1967 and 1971 that delayed escape from codetermination in the event of changes in production or modifications to company structures. Other responses to this legislation included the adoption by companies of new legal forms not covered by the Act and alterations to corporate charters so as to reduce both the frequency and importance of decisions requiring supervisory board approval. A final issue is the possibility that supervisory boards may have been kept deliberately weak by virtue of codetermination.

Empirical analyses of the effects of board representation, the subject of this chapter, have either exploited differences between codetermination and no codetermination or between the various types of codetermination. As we shall see, the early literature revealed few effects of board representation while the subsequent financial literature proved more pessimistic. Latterly, codetermination has received qualified support from a major new financial study and, with the German national innovation debate, from several innovation studies preceded by a panel study of productivity. Before reviewing these findings, however, we must pause to review the theory some of which was touched upon earlier in chapter 3.

7.2 Theoretical Remarks

Some of the material in this section covers familiar ground. The basic starting point is that codetermination is a safeguard for the worker side against opportunistic behavior on the part of employers. Absent some form of protection (either institutional or contractual), so the argument runs, workers will be unwilling to undertake reliance investments such as firm-specific skills acquisition. The upshot is that in circumstances where not all coalition-specific resources are owned by one party, codetermination may provide a governance structure that is capable of dealing with maximizing agents with conflicting interests (Furubotn, 1988, p. 168). However, the codetermination structure envisaged in Furubotn's hypothetical *joint investment firm* where the workers are residual claimants is voluntary. By contrast, under mandatory codetermination major control rights are ceded to workers irrespective of whether or not they have made coalition-specific investments. Further, they are given no income rights in the firm, and normally do not share directly in the residual, and cannot transfer property rights in the job to others, and so on. Politics, so the argument runs, now replace economic responsibility. Workers making decisions do not bear the full cost of their decisions. The situation is to be contrasted with a proper allocation of property rights in the joint investment firm—a sharing of control rights via codetermination—that assures that those making decisions bear the full cost of their actions. This incentive structure promotes both productivity-enhancing incentives as well as relatively lower transaction costs.

Yet, as is self-evident, such voluntary arrangements have not emerged. Why is this? For his part, Furubotn speculates that this is because workers can gain more from the political solution of mandatory codetermination than through private bargaining with the firm. After all, they get up to one-half of the seats on the supervisory board without any corresponding duty to invest.

But the "no-show" result has been exploited more generally by Jensen and Meckling (1976, 1979), who argue that board membership must be detrimental to shareholder value because it has not been embraced by employers. Indeed, they would see the force feeding and strenuous opposition of German employers to parity or quasi-parity codetermination as testimony to their indirect argument as to the inefficiency of mandatory codetermination.

At this point, some of the counterarguments contained in chapter 3 come into play. The starting point is the argument by Levine and Tyson (1990) to the effect that codetermination will be underprovided by the market on prisoner's dilemma grounds. The maintained hypothesis is that codetermination is valuable to all firms but to sustain it a compressed wage structure and dismissals protection are required. In these circumstances, any single innovating firm will suffer an externality and adverse selection: its stars will be spirited away by "traditional" firms, who can offer these workers higher rewards by virtue of their supposedly sharply differentiated wage structures, and it will simultaneously attract the work shy who are now protected from dismissal. On both counts, the codetermined firm will not emerge voluntarily and must be mandated. *Vulgo*: the market is systematically biased against codetermination.

Another line of argument is more compelling because it explicitly recognizes rent seeking on the part of labor. Freeman and Lazear (1995) contend that although codetermination raises the joint surplus it raises the rent going to labor more. Employers duly resist codetermination and it has to be mandated *albeit coupled with institutional limits on the ability of the worker side to extract rents*. The inference of the Freeman-Lazear model (which, it can be recalled from chapter 3, is again constructed around *betriebliche Mitbestimmung*) is that the allocation of control rights to corporate assets may have important implications for economic efficiency but that the absence of the institution outside of a mandate is not necessarily decisive.

Thus far we have assumed an identity of interest between management and shareholders. What if managers are imperfect agents of the shareholder principal? One of the few analyses to exploit such agency considerations is Jirjahn's (2003b) treatment of executive incentives and firm performance. Jirjahn's treatment has a basis in two key associations: first, the relationship between codetermination (in his model it is works council presence rather than worker representation on company boards) and self-enforcing contracts; and, second, the relationship between agency problems and trustful employee relations. An agency problem may have a commitment value in making self-enforcing contracts feasible. But the introduction of profit sharing for managers may give them the incentive to break implicit contracts with the employees on behalf of profit-maximizing owners with adverse consequences for trust. Where codetermination and self-enforcing contracts are substitutes (i.e., the reputation effects mechanism is strong), the impact of codetermination on firm performance will be stronger in firms with less severe agency problems. Since profit sharing reduces agency problems the interaction effect between codetermination and profit sharing for managers will be positive, and hence productive of firm performance. The converse applies where codetermination is complementary to self-enforcing contracts (i.e., reducing the employer's incentive to renege on an implicit agreement) and agency increases the range of self-enforcing contracts.

Next consider active rent seeking in the Jirjahn model. Such behavior on the part of management narrows the range of feasible self-enforcing contracts by impeding cooperative industrial relations. Interaction effects again depend on the relationship between codetermination and self-enforcing contracts in building trust. If they are substitutes, negative interaction effects are expected because, absent managerial profit sharing, codetermination may curb more ambitious rent seeking activities. Any such role for codetermination is attenuated where profit sharing provides an incentive for management to establish trust. Where codetermination and self-enforcing contracts are complementary, on the other hand, the role of codetermination will be more effective in firms with profit sharing.

It follows that there are four possible interaction effects in Jirjahn's model. In fitting a productivity equation to pooled data for 438 German plants observed in 1994 and 1996, he reports that both codetermination and executive profit sharing are positively associated with value-added per employee. But the interaction term is negative. Accordingly, on this model at any rate, either profit sharing reduces the commitment value of agency in situations where codetermination cannot foster trust without the cooperation of management, or management rent seeking is curbed by profit sharing and codetermination is not so important in building cooperation in circumstances of reduced opportunism on the part of management.

The model is ultimately inconclusive, but it is an interesting application of property rights in the context of a contracts model. Although they have largely been neglected, property rights considerations would seem to loom large in the area of worker board representation. To take just one example, inefficient supervisory board structures might dominate diffuse stockholding in circumstances where the alternative is labor-controlled boards.

If Jirjahn's model is firmly set in the framework of *betriebliche Mitbestimmung*, some recent theoretical models have examined board representation more directly in bargaining models (see also chapter 3). In particular, Kraft (2001) considers a model in which shareholders bargain with employee representatives about employment but not wages. In situations of oligopoly, Kraft shows that for some range of bargaining power in this oligopoly model a prisoner's dilemma exists. In short, the firm is better off under a codetermination mandate irrespective of whether other firms are subject to the mandate, and yet all firms are better off if none of them is subject to codetermination (see also Kraft, 1998).[3] Kraft asks whether firms would have an incentive to introduce codetermination voluntarily (if they become aware of the effects in strategic interaction). Here he refers to the "many unfortunate aspects of codetermination" in terms of investment and finance (Kraft, 2001, p. 563). He also notes that codetermination is unlikely to develop naturally given the restriction of the model that bargaining be confined to employment alone.

A final theoretical development of the codetermined firm in oligopoly is offered by Granero (2006), who considers a duopoly model in which one of the firms is a subject to codetermination while its rival is not. He considers the implication of codetermination for R&D and employment. There are two main theoretical results of this strategic R&D model. First, in the absence of bargaining but where there is a utilitarian management, the output best-response function of the codetermined firm shifts out. This can lead the codetermined firm to undertake more R&D investment (and more employment) if the degree of codetermination is "intermediate." Second, where there is bargaining—again over employment but *not* wages that are taken to be exogenous to the firm—the increase in R&D is unambiguous because employment commitments rule out any secondary reduction in employment resulting from the positive effect of R&D on labor productivity. As with Kraft (2001), the relevance of the model ultimately hinges on the nature-of-bargaining assumption but it again serves to demonstrate that theoretical guidance as to the effect of codetermination in not unequivocal.

Finally, since Granero's model alerts us to certain practicalities such as the "threshold value" of codetermination (viz. intermediate rather than high codetermination), what other practicalities of German *Unternehmensmitbestimmung* have to be borne in mind? Corporate control rights in the form of votes are valuable (e.g., by analogy between voting and nonvoting shares) but it is not clear that seats are valuable. Relatedly, and abstracting from the rarity of full-parity representation, only almost-equal representation (rather than one-third representation) may affect firm performance. Further, rent seeking can take a number of forms: codetermination may be used as an intertemporal insurance vehicle protecting workers from adverse shocks and more generally by limiting shareholder's flexibility. And if the U.S. *union* literature is applicable, shareholders for their part may take countervailing measures. They might increase firm leverage or they might even seek to change the remuneration of the supervisory board. It follows from these practicalities that investigation of the consequences of enterprise codetermination is a multifaceted exercise.

7.3 The Evidence

7.3.1 *Initial Findings*

The early literature suggested that codetermination at enterprise level had minimal impact on firm performance. Thus, using different data and methodologies, Svejnar (1981), Benelli, Loderer, and Lys (1987), and Gurdon and Rai (1990) each concluded that the introduction of the 1951, 1952, and 1976 Acts had minimal impact on corporate performance. As far as *Montanmitbestimmung* is concerned, in comparing two industries subject to parity codetermination with the textile industry Svejnar (1981) found that the introduction of codetermination was associated with significantly higher relative earnings in one (iron and steel) but not the other (bituminous coal mining) (see also Svejnar, 1982). Benelli, Loderer, and Lys (1987) report that the variance in annual stock returns in industries subject to full-parity codetermination was lower than in other in other industries, 1954–1976, suggesting less risky investments were being undertaken. But the difference between the two-digit industry groups was not statistically significant.

Turning to the 1976 Act, Benelli, Loderer, and Lys in an examination of monthly portfolio return variances in 40 codetermined firms (and 18 noncodetermined firms) over a period before and after passage of the 1976 Act report a decline in variance. But the same was true of the noncodetermined firm sample. And average monthly stock returns dipped in both sets of firms prior to the passage of the Act. Similarly, analysis of differences in means among matched pairs of codetermined and noncodetermined firms over an interval preceding and following passage of the legislation indicated no statistically significant differences in leverage, profitability, dividend payout, capital intensity, and labor costs. Finally, in an analysis of variance, Gurdon and Rai (1990) report materially higher profitability (but lower productivity) in their sample of codetermined firms post-1976 than for the control group (of 26 firms).

7.3.2 A Pessimistic Intermezzo?

Each of the above studies has come in for trenchant criticism for reasons that include sample size, data frequency (in the case of stock returns), lack of controls for other relevant economic or organizational variables, focus on a single event, and narrow reach. The next phase of research sought to remedy these shortcomings, and in the process offered an altogether more pessimistic view of *Unternehmensmitbestimmung*.

The first study identified here is notable for its use of a larger sample of firms (but see below) and regression framework. FitzRoy and Kraft (1993) estimate translog production functions for a sample of 112 firms using two cross-sections of data for 1975 and 1983, namely the last year before passage of the 1976 Act and an "equivalent" (i.e., recession) year sufficiently long after event for the law to have taken effect. The analysis hinges on the 68 firms that had over 2,000 employees in both years and therefore changed their codetermination status from one-third to quasi-party codetermination. In each cross-section, the dummy variable COD identifies firms with 2,000 or more employees, so that the change in the point estimate identifies the effect of the change in the law.[4]

The authors run three sets of regressions for each cross-section: value-added, total labor cost per employee, and return on equity. In a final regression, they consider the determinants of productivity growth, 1975–1983. The value-added regressions record a statistically significant positive coefficient estimate for COD in 1975 and an insignificantly negative coefficient estimate for 1983. The difference between the two coefficient estimates is statistically significant at the 0.10 level. That said, the labor cost regressions do not suggest that wages increased, even though the COD coefficient estimates were significantly positive in both years. Yet return on equity *did* decline significantly over the two years, while the total factor productivity equation indicated that the move to quasi-parity codetermination was associated with a reduction in growth.

This was the first study to suggest that the shift to quasi-parity codetermination after 1976 might have measurable private costs: a productivity loss of just under 20 percent of value-added. Yet the rent seeking mechanism does not appear to be wages but rather "increased job security and immobility" (FitzRoy and Kraft, 1993, p. 374) (see also chapter 4).

Results consistent with those found by FitzRoy and Kraft are reported by Schmid and Seger (1998) in a German language study of a sample of 160 large publicly traded companies observed in 1976, 1987, and 1991. (We will abstract from that part of the authors' study dealing with voting blocks in company meetings and revisit this issue below in the final Phase 2 analysis considered here.) The dependent variable in this regression study is the market-to-book ratio of equity and the comparison group is again firms with one-third employee representation. Unlike FitzRoy and Kraft (1993), however, this study does not contrast the performance of a given firm before and after the passage of legislation but instead pools the observations and uses year dummies (for 1987 and 1991) and control variables specific to the firm to net out the effects of codetermination. The coefficient estimate for COD implies an 18 percent decline in share prices. As the authors put it, shareholders would have been willing to cede around 22 percent of the current value of their prelegislation investment to cancel that legislation, where this "willingness to pay" is the market price of the loss of control rights experienced by shareholders.

The next study examined here by Baums and Frick (1998) is of interest for several reasons. First is an events study using daily stock return data. Second, it examines over a period of more than 20 years (January 1, 1974 through December 1995), the outcome of 23 court decisions concerning application of the 1976 Act, either extending or restricting codetermination. (The cases in question were either litigated by the relevant industrial union or by firms seeking to reject the union's claims.) In other words, the sample arguably identifies those cases most likely to suffer material loss as a result of passage of the 1976 Act. Third, the findings of the study are more in line with the earlier literature.

Familiarly, the authors compute abnormal returns and the sum of abnormal returns (or cumulated abnormal returns) for the 28 firms in question.[5] The authors consider the abnormal returns on the event days—the date the judicial decision was issued—as well as cumulated abnormal returns in the 10 days before and after the event (plus a variety of longer-event windows), and also present regression estimates inter alia of the contribution of the type of decision reached (extension/restriction), the outcome (firm wins, union wins, or neither wins), the type of court involved (court of first instance, Appellate Court, Federal Civil Court, Federal Constitutional Court) and reach or ambit of the decision (affecting the firm only or having an economy-wide impact).

Baums and Frick report that abnormal returns on the event day were modestly positive and were larger (smaller) where there was an extension (restriction) of codetermination rights, although in neither case were these changes statistically significant. Cumulated abnormal returns evinced no pattern, and were not systematically related to type of decision. Nor for that matter did company success (or failure) lead to an increase (decrease) in abnormal returns on either the event day or thereafter. Turning to the authors' regression analysis, in no case were the structural characteristics of the court decision statistically significant determinants of the abnormal return or the cumulated abnormal return.

This issue of "employer friendly" and "employee friendly" legal decisions offers a highly innovative approach to determining the consequences of codetermination. The fact that the authors were unable to find statistically significant stock market reactions to the verdicts, one way or another, is intriguing. But Baums and Frick do, however, offer two possible reasons for their finding that stockholders did not experience financial losses due to legal decisions that extended codetermination rights. First a technical reason: the judgment dates used did not correspond to the (unobserved in this study) announcement dates on which information about the disputes or lawsuits was disseminated in the press. In short, the results may have been an artifact of the data, hiding real losses of stockholders. Second, the judicial decisions observed may not have been that important. More important in this respect perhaps were the dates corresponding to the introduction of the Act (July 1, 1976) and the ruling of the Federal Constitutional Court that the Act was constitutional (March 1, 1979). Acting against this latter interpretation, however, is the authors' separate sectoral analysis that fails generally to detect negative (positive) changes in average abnormal returns in the sectors most (least) impacted by the Act, comparing the two-and-a-half year period prior to the introduction of the Act/declaration of its constitutionality and the 10 days thereafter.

The final study of this phase of the literature by Gorton and Schmid (2004) still represents perhaps the most detailed study to date of the effects of codetermination on firm financial performance. It reaches fairly strong conclusions that are more in keeping with the U.S. *union* literature (e.g., Hirsch, 1991, Chapter 4) other than in one important respect. Gorton and Schmid examine the consequences of codetermination for the largest 250 nonfinancial traded stock corporations in Germany using a pooled cross-section time-series data for the sample period 1989–1993. They consider in turn whether quasi-parity codetermination (as compared with one-third representation) affects the performance of the firm—and the manner of that influence—and whether, as reported in the U.S. literature, shareholders responded by taking countervailing measures (such as the assumption of increased debt) to offset the influence of the worker board members.

The authors pay especial attention to the ownership structure of the German corporation and to the monitoring function. Some relevant distinguishing characteristics of the German governance system to keep in mind here are the importance of block share holding, and the role of the banks in controlling equity and corporate governance. Also relevant is the composition of the supervisory board where one-third of shareholder representatives have no equity interest in the company and where the labor side consists of several groups (the most important of which are workers who are not affiliated with unions or works councils, labor union representatives, and middle management). Finally, as far as ownership structure is concerned, the German situation is complicated because of pyramiding and cross-shareholding. This brings about a distinction between cash flow rights and control rights. In their study, Gorton and Schmid thus use the notion of "ultimate ownership." And ultimate ownership emerges as highly concentrated. In their estimating equations, the authors control for the equity control rights held by three types of (ultimate) owners that have been found in the literature to affect the stock market performance of the firm: government, banks, and insiders. They also control for shareholder concentration through the size of the largest existing stake of equity control rights, using a categorical variable.

In analyzing the effect of codetermination on the economic performance of the firm, Gorton and Schmid use two forward-looking financial indicators: the market-to-book ratio of equity (MTB) and Tobin's q (i.e., the market value of the firm divided by the replacement cost of assets). But, as noted earlier, they range much further afield and also examine the effects of codetermination on company leverage, the wage bill-to-employees ratio, the employee-to-sales ratio, and the compensation of the management board and the supervisory board.

Beginning with financial performance, their econometric estimation proceeds using a regression discontinuity approach. Familiarly, the principal codetermination regressor picks up the effect of quasi-parity representation versus one-third representation. The authors present semiparametric regression estimates for (logarithmic) MTB for each of the five years 1989–1993. In each case, the coefficient estimate for COD is negative and statistically significant. The stock market discount ranges from 21 percent in 1989 to 43 percent in 1992, averaging 31 percent over the period. In short, going from one-third to almost-equal worker representation appears to have very serious consequences for shareholder wealth, seemingly providing the context of the strong opposition of German employers to the 1976 legislation noted in our introduction.

Apart from codetermination, the second most important influence on this profit measure is the fraction of control rights exercised by the government! A 1 percentage point increase in this fraction decreases the stock market valuation of the firm by between 0.26 and 0.41 percent. On the other hand, the effect of insiders on performance is generally positive. In other words, the greater the equity control rights held by management, other employees, and families, the better is financial performance. The influence of the other regressors is mixed.

Gorton and Schmid then check the robustness of their main results. They first reestimate the regression discontinuity model substituting Tobin's q for MTB and then deploy a nearest-neighbor approach using both performance indicators. Use of Tobin's q yields a narrow spread of statistically significant negative effects of quasi-parity codetermination in the range 24–29 percent, and averaging 26 percent 1989–1993. Use of a nearest-neighbor (peer group or single firm) approach yields a smaller discount in the range 9–15 percent.[6]

The balance of the authors' analysis is given over to investigating whether codetermination alters the objective function of the firm and possible shareholder countermeasures. In seeking an answer to the former question, Gorton and Schmid first examine the effects of board representation on managerial compensation before turning to inquire into labor's objectives more directly through regressions in which the dependent variables are the ratio of the wage bill to the number of employees, the ratio of employees to sales, and the wage bill-to-sales ratio. The upshot of the authors' nearest-neighbor analysis of managerial compensation is that average management board compensation is contemporaneously negatively linked to performance (measured by MTB) in quasi-parity codetermined firms, and conversely for their counterparts with one-third worker board membership. As far as labor's objectives are concerned, the authors' regression discontinuity estimates point to an absence of any effect of codetermination on the ratio of the (log) wage bill to the number of employees. This result is attributed by the authors to a wage determination process that is conducted outside the firm at industry or regional level. But if codetermination has no measurable impact on earnings, material effects are reported for employment, alternatively measured as the (log) ratio of employees to sales and the (log) ratio of the wage bill to sales. Averaged over each of the five years in the sample period, codetermination is associated with a 48 percent longer payroll and a 55 percent higher payroll. The implication is that codetermination results in overstaffing and success by the worker side in altering the objective function of the firm.[7]

In the final part of their analysis, Gorton and Schmid examine whether shareholders take countermeasures that limit—presumably at some cost—worker appropriation of the firm's surplus. Using their nearest-neighbors approach, they report that shareholders respond to quasi-parity representation by increasing the performance sensitivity of supervisory board compensation. That is to say, the pay of nonexecutive directors is more sensitive to firm performance when workers have quasi-parity board representation than when one-third of the board is made up of worker representatives. In the spirit of the U.S. union literature, the authors also test whether leverage is higher under quasi-parity representation. Their regression discontinuity estimates indicate that the effect of equal representation is to increase the debt-equity ratio by between 47 and 81 percent over the sample period, or by 69 percent on average. Accordingly, Gorton and Schmid (2004, p. 895) conclude: "Shareholders attempt to align with shareholder wealth the interests of employer representatives on the supervisory board by linking employer compensation to firm performance and by leveraging up the firm."

Summarizing the literature up to this point, we observe that the anodyne results from the widely criticized early studies have given way to cet. par. estimates that tend to paint a much bleaker picture of the economic consequences of codetermination at board level. But, as is so often the case with studies of German institutions, a revisionist interpretation is actively under way.

7.3.3 A Rehabilitation of Quasi-Parity Codetermination?

The term "rehabilitation" appears apropos in discussing the analysis of FitzRoy and Kraft (2005), who revisit their earlier finding that the 1976 Act adversely impacted labor productivity (although they do not investigate whether the same holds true for firm profitability—but see below—and the other indicators examined in FitzRoy and Kraft, 1993). The authors now seek to control for unobserved firm heterogeneity or firm-specific effects, necessarily neglected in their cross-section study.

Using panel data for 179 manufacturing firms from 1972–1976 and 1981–1985 (i.e., pre- and post-1976 panels), they regress (log) sales on a codetermination dummy defined as firm size greater than or equal to 2,000 (i.e., COD) in both panels and an additional codetermination dummy defined as codetermined firms only after 1980 (i.e., COD80). The latter variable thus picks up the effect of moving form one-third to quasi-parity codetermination, while the former variable is now designed to control for any possible size effect present in the 2,000 employee limit. Other regressors are labor, capital, material inputs, overtime hours, concentration, and imports and exports. Since conventional firm fixed effects cannot be distinguished from codetermination effects, the authors' proceed by allowing some of the other explanatory variables to be related to firm-specific effects and others not, using the Hausman-Taylor (1981) method in which both codetermination variables are instrumented. The authors' Cobb-Douglas production function estimates suggest that the switch from one-third to quasi-parity codetermination raised productivity somewhat; specifically, by less than 1 percent. An alternative specification also allowing for the effect of one-third representation prior to 1976, defined as firms with more than 500 but less than 2,000 employees, produced similar results for the change to almost-equal parity representation (although the omitted category now comprises very much smaller firms than before) and a positive coefficient estimate for the new codetermination dummy (subject of course to the caveat than no before-and-after test is employed here). On net, the authors conclude that they can now reject the view that the 1976 Act had effects that were primarily redistributional.

Kraft and Ugarković (2006) basically repeat the exercise for the "missing dependent variable": the rate of return on equity. That is, their estimations use panel data for 179 companies from 1971–1976 and from 1981 to 1986 using the Hausman-Taylor approach. The regressors include a quadratic in establishment size, capital intensity, market share, the six-firm concentration ratio, export and import shares, extent of overtime working, and three age dummies—and, in one specification by way of a robustness check, a dummy variable for those firms with one-third worker board representation throughout (although this does not allow them to recoup a before-and-after outcome for this lesser-codetermination argument). The authors' fitted Hausman-Taylor model suggests the additional effect of the introduction of parity codetermination to the initial difference between potential parity codetermination firms and the rest was a small positive value implying a modestly favorable impact on the return on equity of the 1976 strengthening in the codetermination law.

Analysts thus far have neglected the issue of investment that is something of a missing link in the study of codetermination and allocative efficiency. With the national innovation debate in Germany (see *Nationales Reformprogramm Deutschland*, 2005), however, the role of company boards in influencing intangible capital has attracted some scrutiny. To date there have been just two innovation studies, both using patents as the output indicator and building on the theoretical models of strategic R&D introduced in section 6.2. Kraft, Stank, and Dewenter (2003), in an analysis of patent data for 1971–1990 covering 162 stock companies (62 of which were codetermined after 1976), report evidence of modestly higher R&D activity (around 4 percent) among codetermined firms. A similar result is found by Kraft and Stank (2004).

But we lack studies of investment. Even if none of the studies reviewed here has obtained evidence of higher wages under quasi-parity codetermination, several have pointed to lower profitability that may adversely impact investment in imperfect capital markets. In the interstices, it is also worth noting here that although patents might be expected to exhibit a relationship with codetermination largely similar to that obtaining in the case of R&D inputs, codetermined companies may patent, given their innovation capital, as a means of reducing rent appropriation. As pointed out in the U.S. union literature, patents offer the opportunity for firms to license product and process innovations, to transform what might otherwise be firm-specific innovative capital into general capital and thereby lessen any ability on the part of the employee side on the supervisory board to appropriate the quasi-rents from that capital (see Hirsch, 2004).

We conclude this review with two very recent studies that provide stronger results: the first by Renaud (2007) is very much in the spirit of FitzRoy and Kraft (2005)/Kraft and Ugarković (2006); and the second by Fauver and Fuerst (2006) is very much a companion study to Gorton and Schmid (2004). We begin with Renaud's very recent analysis of 250–500 companies from the German Financial Database, 1970–2000, which uses the dummies COD and COD80 and the Hausman-Taylor approach. Renaud provides three sets of regressions. The first offers a difference-in-differences analysis of value-added and profits in which 1970–1976 is the pretreatment period and 1980–2000 is the posttreatment period.[8] The second seeks to determine the effects of parity codetermination over time using differences in the *trends* of productivity and profits in near-parity codetermined firms and the rest of the sample with one-third employee board representation. The third is a changing parameters model combining elements of the two former approaches. The regressors in the productivity model in addition to the two codetermination variables are employment, capital, age dummies, unit labor costs, and time and industry dummies. The profits equation adds capital intensity and the debt ratio as regressors.

The results are as follows. The basic difference-in-differences regression points to mixed coefficients estimates for COD but positive and statistically significant estimates for COD80, suggesting that the introduction of near-parity codetermination increased both productivity and profitability in the affected companies in the wake of the 1976 law.[9] The trend estimates of productivity and profitability are mixed. Thus, there is no suggestion of any differential productivity growth favoring quasi-parity codetermined firms after 1980, or indeed any initial differences between the two sets of firms. For profitability, the initial difference is actually negative and statistically significant but the trend interaction terms indicate that the profitability situation for quasi-parity codetermined firms improved after 1980 relative to the control group. As far as the evolution of the trend is concerned, the author obtains no differential effects in any year after 1980 for productivity while in the case of profitability just one interaction term (for the most recent year) is positive and well determined. For both trend analyses, the author cautions that any observed trend differences between the two groups of firms may have resulted from other, unobserved influences on productivity and profits not captured by the model's controls. So perhaps the most reasonable conclusion from this study after all is that codetermined companies did not suffer from the 1976 law.

This brings us in conclusion to the important study by Fauver and Fuerst (2006) in which it is argued that *prudent levels of employee representation* on company boards can improve board level decision making. It is further argued that the potential payoff can be expected to be greater in industries requiring more intense coordination and information-sharing activities, and that the presence of labor representatives can enhance the monitoring of managers and thereby reduce shirking activities. No such favorable inferences are drawn with respect to union representation on company boards.[10]

Fauver and Fuerst examine a larger sample of firms than do Gorton and Schmid, including firms without any employee board representation, albeit for 2003 alone. The sample consists of *all* publicly held firms traded on the German stock exchange at that time (n = 786). The authors present a series of cross-sectional regressions using Tobin's *q*, supplemented with logit regressions of dividend payments. In addition to the key labor representation measure—namely the presence of one or more employee board level representatives—the covariates include firm size, business segment, geographic diversification, ownership concentration, bank board members, industry concentration, leverage (total debt divided by total assets), and several interaction terms.

In the initial regressions, the key employee representation indicator has no effect on firm value as measured by Tobin's *q*. However, when interacted with industries purportedly requiring greater coordination, labor involvement, and more specialized employee skills sets (together *process complexity*) the coefficient estimate for the interaction term is positive and statistically significant throughout. Voluntary representation, captured by a variable that takes the value of one where the number of employee representatives exceeds the legal limits, always has a positive influence on shareholder value. By the same token, union representation is uniformly insignificant.[11]

As far as ownership concentration, industrial diversification, and industrial concentration are concerned, employee representation offsets negative effects and amplifies positive effects on shareholder value. For example, employee board members appear to monitor and reduce the appropriation of small shareholders by powerful blockholders who would otherwise govern the firm to maximize their own private benefit.

Returning to the point that industries requiring more intense coordination, integration of activities, and information-sharing benefit more from codetermination, there is some indication that employee representation that "weakly exceeds one-third percent but is strictly less than 50 percent" in interaction with these industry indicators (e.g., trade, manufacturing, and transportation) evinces a positive and statistically significant effect on firm value while all other employee representation levels (0–33 percent and > 50 percent) prove statistically insignificant. Accordingly, Fauver and Fuerst speak of there being some optimal level of representation.

Finally, the authors claim they are able to reproduce Gorton and Schmid's (2004) results when they restrict the sample to the top 250 companies and use these authors' measure of employee representation (i.e., quasi-parity representation = 1, 0 otherwise) and controls. They conclude therefore that the difference between the two studies reflects (1) sample size considerations, (2) the greater likelihood of union representatives as opposed to true employees being on company boards in the Gorton-Schmid sample, and (3) the interaction of complex and high coordination industries and employee board representation neglected Gorton and Schmid.

7.4 Conclusions

Worker representation on company boards arouses strong feelings. At one extreme it is viewed as tantamount to wealth confiscation (e.g., Alchian, 1984, p. 46) with palpably adverse consequences for firm performance. At another, it is viewed as helping guarantee cooperative labor relations, with long-term gains in terms of productivity and improved worker morale. Intermediate positions would recognize the joint occurrence of allocative and distributive effects, permitting either increases or decreases in overall welfare (according to the position taken on the ability of the German system to mediate the conflict between the two forces).

The official German position would appear to be that codetermination is an essential element of the *social* market economy. But, as we discovered in chapter 2, opinions of the main interest groups (if not public opinion) in Germany are sharply divided on the efficacy of near-parity codetermination: employer organizations seeking a ratcheting back to one-third codetermination *as a default position* and the unions wanting an extension (reducing the threshold for quasi-parity codetermination from 2,000 to 1,000 employees). The process of globalization and European mandates in this area (see chapter 8) ensure that this debate will continue, even if 82 percent of the German public seemingly favors the status quo ante as regards the codetermination rights of employees in supervisory boards (Hans Böckler Stiftung, 2005).

In the present chapter we have considered the arguments for and against worker representation on the supervisory board. Theory offers guidance but does not allow an unequivocal position to be taken on the issue, absent very stringent assumptions. As usual, therefore, we were led to consider the empirical evidence. This material is quite simply fascinating and displays the many twists and turns by now familiar in German research, plus it has to be said a *soupçon* of political correctness.

We traced three phases of a still sparse literature. The first, comprising a mix of event studies and nonparametric analyses, failed to detect any systematic effect of board codetermination on firm performance. The widely recognized limitations of this research led to a second phase of research comprising econometric studies and events analyses containing controls lacking in the earlier literature and richer stock market data. Although the evidence from this second phase is not uniform—for example, an innovative events study of those firms most likely to be favored/disfavored by the 1976 legislation fails to chart corresponding movements in shareholder value—the balance of the evidence suggests that codetermination is associated with lower productivity, lower profits, a lower market-to-book ratio of equity (and q-ratio), higher labor costs (if not wages), longer payrolls, and some suggestion of shareholder countermeasures. Finally, the most recent literature provides several reversals of finding and several new results. First, there is the suggestion that the negative productivity and profitability effects observed in the second phase literature may be artefacts of cross-section estimation. Second, there is the suggestion that innovation as measured by patents may be modestly higher in codetermination regimes. Both are interesting findings even if the innovation result may not be particularly compelling until supported by similar evidence on R&D inputs. But most intriguing of all are the findings of the two modern financial studies of the market value of the firm. They hold out the prospect that good corporate governance might include employee representation by virtue of the monitoring function and the reduction in agency costs. But equally, one of the studies in particular raises important caveats concerning the extent of employee representation and the role of external, union representatives.

This, then, is the current state of play in the board level codetermination literature. Further progress in this area would seem to await more detailed analysis of German corporate governance, tantalizing glimpses into which are offered by both the theory and the more detailed of the extant financial studies. And at some stage investigation of the interaction between board membership and works councils needs to be attempted, which is not an easy assignment given the size thresholds of even one-third employee representation and the strong direct association between works council presence and establishment size. The public debate needs to be better informed by research findings than has generally been the case,[12] including, it has to be said, those awkward issues raised by research otherwise favorable to worker representation on company boards.

CHAPTER 8

European Rules for Informing and Consulting Employees and the European Dimension

8.1 Introduction

In this final substantive chapter, we examine European level rules on informing and consulting workers and the European dimension. At first blush, the template for much European legislation appears to be the German or *Rhenish* model. Is this erection of German-style worker information and consultation to be construed as the working out of a process of regulatory capture in which countries with more ambitious (and costly?) models seek to raise their less-regulated rivals' costs by forcing them to adopt analogous rules? Or is the process altogether more complex than this, masking conflicting positions of labor and capital out of which individual government positions are fashioned in often complex national political arrangements? These are the crucial issues examined in the present chapter. The European dimension is important precisely because national law in Germany no less than in the other member states is increasing driven by European Union initiatives.

In what follows, we first present a history of EU legislation as it pertains to works councils and worker directors, broadly interpreted. We next argue that works council-type laws follow a German template because of the broad acceptance by German employers (and others) of worker representation at establishment level whereas their resistance to quasi-parity representation has made them allies with other employer groups from countries with more liberal traditions. At least from an employer perspective there is every indication that German interests are not served by upward harmonization—namely, the erection of ever-tighter Community laws in these areas—because the more pressing need is perceived to be changing the system and not shoring up the status quo ante.

But it would be idle to claim that the European dimension is settled. For example, the first major piece of legislation considered here—the European Works Council Directive—was adopted in 1994 and slated for revision in September 1999, but it is only in recent months that the European Commission has been able to frame a new draft directive. And in the case of the second piece of legislation considered, the 2001 European Company Statute, that legislation had first been proposed somewhat more than 30 years earlier. Yet, if past experience is any guide, the march of upward harmonization however protracted and subject to fits and starts is likely to continue in Europe. But it will probably fall well short of mandating worker directors because shareholder value has for a number of years now been winning ground as an ideology. Arguably, as part of a contrary tendency, unions in many member states, not least Germany, will find common cause in seeking more intrusive legislation, irrespective of the consequences for their organizational base.

8.2 The Development of Systems for Informing and Consulting Workers in the European Union

8.2.1 In the Beginning...

Active social policy in the European Community, as it then was, can be traced back to October 1972 when a summit meeting of the heads of state of member nations of the EC gave support to a vigorous social policy having the same importance as the achievement of economic union. In response, the European Commission—the body responsible for proposing Community legislation—put forward an ambitious social action plan that proposed mandates in the areas of health and safety at work, minimum wages, working hours, employee participation and the hiring of contract labor (Commission, 1974).

Success was to be limited given the absence of a firm treaty basis for policy and diversity of practice among member states. Where the Commission did not stray far from the latter it achieved modest success in securing three directives to strengthen worker job rights in circumstances of collective redundancies (i.e., mass layoffs), transfers of undertakings, and firm insolvencies.[1] All three measures established information and consultation procedures in respect of affected workers. Similar procedures were required under separate health and safety legislation—11 such directives were adopted between 1978 and 1987—although here the divergence with national practice was more fundamental but political sensitivity greater (Addison and Siebert, 1991).

But if there were successes in essentially "marginal" rules pertaining to information, consultation, and participation, impasse was reached on more direct measures of this genre. Thus, the "Vredeling initiative," the European Company Statute (ECS), and the draft Fifth Directive on Company Law were to remain deadlocked in Council. Vredeling (introduced in 1980 and amended in 1983 to raise the size threshold from 100 to 1,000 employees) called for employees of multinational corporations to be given information on a wide range of economic, financial, business, and employment issues plus consultation on decisions likely to affect their interests.[2] The two other proposals went much further. The European Company Statute (ECS) provided for worker representation on the supervisory boards of companies that *elected* to become a "European Company" and thereby take advantage of a unified legal system and certain interim tax advantages.[3] Finally, the draft Fifth Company Directive also proposed obligatory worker directors on the supervisory boards of all public corporations employing more than 500 employees. It was modified by the Commission in 1983 to take account of unitary or monistic board structures and in principle to allow for a wider range of participation options—employee election to the supervisory boards, the creation of a separate consultation body made up of employee representatives but having the same rights to information as the supervisory board, and a collectively bargained arrangement corresponding to the principles of the other models.[4] Here, and in all other areas (atypical worker directives and parental leave) where unanimity was required in Council, the Commission confronted strong opposition when it strayed too far from existing custom and practice.

The next phase of Community policy—the social charter—was ushered in by the 1986 Single European Act (SEA). Hitherto unanimity had been required in Council. Now, qualified majority voting was introduced as a quid pro quo for measures accelerating the removal of obstacles to competition, leading to completion of the internal market. Just two years after the implementation of the SEA the Community was to issue a solemn proclamation of fundamental social rights—the *social charter*—in December 1989 (Commission, 1989a). Draft legislation followed swiftly, the hallmark of which was the creative use of health and safety criterion under Article 118A of the treaty. No less than 47 separate initiatives were foreshadowed by the charter's social action program of which 23 called for binding legislation (Commission, 1989b). One of the most controversial items on the commission's shopping list was a draft directive seeking to set up transnational works councils. (Note that in a 1975 revision of the ECS it had earlier been proposed that a directly elected European Works Council be set up in all companies with at least two establishments in different member states with at least 50 employees.) But the measure was blocked by a British veto.

8.2.2 The European Works Council Directive

In the light of British opposition, this EWC directive was instead to be pursued under the *Agreement on Social Policy*. That is, there were now to be two sets of rules governing social policy in the new EU: the standard treaty route under which Commission proposals would be processed before all member states and the Agreement on Social Policy excluding the British (see Addison and Siebert, 1994).[5] The Agreement on Social Policy contained two major innovations concerning treaty basis (or competence) and the process of social dialogue. Beginning with the former, the Agreement confirmed and clarified the legal competence of the Community in matters of social policy while extending the basis of qualified majority voting. Specifically, it set down five areas where qualified majority voting would apply—one of which covered the information and consultation rights of workers—and another five areas that would continue to require unanimity. The second innovation was the role reserved for the two sides of industry—the "social partners"—at European level.[6] Prior to framing proposals in the social policy field, the Commission had to consult the social partners on the possible direction of Community action. Following such consultation, if the Commission decided to pursue legislation, it had again to consult the social partners on the proposed details. At any stage in these second-stage negotiations the social partners could inform the Commission that they would like to negotiate on the issue. At their joint request, any resulting framework agreements could be implemented (i.e., given the force of law) by a Council decision following on a proposal from the Commission.

Indeed, the first use of this Agreement on Social Policy route was the proposal for transnational works councils. As a practical matter, the social partners were not able to reach agreement on the measure and so the Commission presented its own proposals that were adopted in Council in September 1994.[7] Transnational or European Works Councils were to be set up in undertakings with at least 1,000 employees in the member states and at least 150 employees in each of at least

2 member states. A special negotiating body (SNB) of elected worker representatives was to negotiate the information and consultation powers of the works council (or information and consultation procedure) with central management. To trigger negotiations required the written request of at least 100 workers or their representatives in at least 2 undertakings or at least 2 establishments in at least 2 different member states, unless management initiated the negotiations. The SNB could decide on a two-thirds majority not to open negotiations, or to end them. If negotiations were successfully concluded, there were no minimum requirements as such, although the agreement had to cover the scope, composition, membership, and powers of the EWC together with the financial and material resources to be allocated by management to the EWC as well as the duration of the agreement and the procedure for its renegotiation. (The two parties might instead decide to establish one or more information and consultation procedures in lieu of a EWC that had nevertheless to cover transnational issues.)

In the event that the SNB and central management failed to reach agreement, certain "subsidiary requirements" of statutory EWCs were to apply. In particular, the directive stipulated that meetings between the EWC and management must be held at least once a year and cover "the structure, economic and financial situation, the probable development of the business and of production and sales, the situation and trend of employment, investments, and substantial changes concerning organization, introduction of new working methods or production processes, transfers of production, mergers, cut-backs or closures of undertakings, establishments or important parts thereof, and collective redundancies." Where exceptional circumstances arose, the EWC or a select committee of the EWC had the right to be informed. It was to have the right to meet at its request the central management, or any more appropriate level of management, so as to be informed and consulted on measures significantly affecting members' interests.

Member states had two years (until September 22 1996) to implement the directive. In the interstices, employers could conclude preemptive agreements (under Article 13 of the directive). Such Article 13 agreements covering the entire labor force and providing for transnational information and consultation of the latter escaped the obligations of the directive. However, upon expiry the directive's terms and conditions would apply unless the parties chose to renew them.

The 1994 directive is currently in the process of revision following abortive negotiations between the social partners in April 2008. As noted earlier, the Commission has already issued a draft directive revising the directive.[8] These proposals will bring the EWC statute more into line with the next two pieces of legislation described below, as well as amendments to updated Commission initiatives on collective redundancies and transfers of undertakings covering worker information and consultation rights.[9]

8.2.3 The European Company Statute

Abstracting from the employment chapter (see Addison, 2008), the hallmark of the next phase of Community social policy (ushered in by the 1997 Treaty of Amsterdam, which incorporated the provisions on the Agreement on Social Policy directly into the main body of the treaty, so that it became a *social chapter* after all) was the passage of two more pieces of legislation dealing with worker involvement in their companies (see Commission, 2000).

Of these the more important was the European Company Statute, adopted in October 2001 after some 30 years of "revisions, impasses and revivals" (EIRR, 2002, p. 21). The legislation pertains to the *voluntary* incorporation of an entity—via conversion of an existing public limited company,[10] merger, the setting up of a joint holding company, or the creation of a joint subsidiary—as a European Company, or *Societas Europaea* (SE), thereby benefiting from a simplified financial and tax regime.[11] Incorporation carries with it rules for employee involvement that are identified in a draft directive. (The legislation is in two parts: a Regulation dealing with the company law aspects and an employee involvement directive addressed here.)[12]

Similar to the EWC, under the directive central management has to negotiate with a special negotiating body (SNB) composed of worker representatives with the aim of reaching a written agreement on the terms of worker involvement. Unlike the EWC legislation, however, the proposals set down specific formulae for SNB representation and also reserve an explicit role for trade unions on the SNB. (In each case, member states are to determine the rules for the election or appointment of SNB members in their territories.) The proposals also contain various options for qualified majority voting within the SNB on several important issues even if majority voting applies in the normal run of events. For example, a qualified majority of two-thirds is required for a decision on the part of the SNB not to open negotiations or to terminate negotiations already in progress—in which case the parties simply rely on the national rules on information and consultation in the respective member states (although this option is not available where the SE is created by the transformation of a single company if that company already has board level participation arrangements).

The goal of the directive is information provision, consultation, and, ultimately, participation. Where the SNB engages in negotiations, the options are threefold: a written agreement on employee involvement arrangements, an agreement to apply the directive's statutory standard rules, and application of the latter as a default where there is failure to reach an agreement within a specified time interval. Written agreements have to cover information and consultation either through a "representative body" or through one or more information and consultation procedures. Where a representative body is set up, the agreement has to specify its composition, number of members, and allocation of seats. It has further to stipulate the functions of the body and the procedures for informing and consulting it, the frequency of meetings, and the financial resources to be allocated. If instead the parties agree on the other option, the agreement has to specify the arrangements for implementing these other procedures. For their part, any *participation* arrangements must specify the substance of the board level arrangements. In SEs established by the transformation of a single EU-based company, board participation is not optional in the sense that the agreement must fix the same level of involvement as previously applied. And in those (other) cases where the agreement reduces board level participation below the highest level applying in the participative companies, this has to be approved by a qualified majority vote of SNB members.

The directive's standard rules that apply by agreement or default provide for information and consultation through a representative body and in some circumstances for board level representation. In the case of information and consultation, the standard rules cover both the composition of the representative body and detailed requirements as to their information and consultation. The latter are largely the same (actually modestly higher) as for EWCs.

The rules on board membership are differentiated by type of SE (i.e., the manner in which it was formed). They do not apply if none of the participating companies were governed by board level representation prior to formation of the SE, whereas if the SE was established by the transformation of an existing company a member state's rules on board level participation simply carry over to the SE. In SEs established by setting up a joint holding company or subsidiary the standard rules apply if one or more forms of board level representation previously covered at least 50 percent of the total workforce of the entity—or, if less, at the discretion of the SNB. Finally, in the case of SEs established by merger, the standard rules would apply if at least 25 percent of the total workforce of the constituent companies had earlier been covered—or, where less, again if the SNB so decides. In this particular case, however, the member state can choose not to apply the standard rules on board level representation.[13] In each of the three instances (i.e., for cases other than an SE being formed by transformation) the standard rules call for the appointment of members of the administrative or supervisory board in an amount equal to the highest proportion in force in the participating companies obtaining prior to registration.

8.2.4 On a General Framework for Informing and Consulting Workers

The second piece of legislation—adopted in March 2002 some four years after it was first mooted—establishes a general framework to be followed in informing and consulting employees in Community undertakings with at least 50 employees in any one member state or establishments employing at least 20 employees in any one member state (as determined by the member state).[14] Both information and consultation are defined in terms of their timing and efficacy.

Information covers the recent and probable development of the undertaking's/establishment's activities and economic situation. It is to be given in timely fashion, enabling employees' representatives to conduct an adequate investigation and, where necessary, prepare for consultation. The employer has also to inform and consult on the situation, structure, and probable development of employment within the entity and on any anticipatory measures envisaged, particularly where there is a threat to employment. Information and consultation are required for decisions likely to lead to substantial changes work organization or in contractual relations, including those covered by legislation pertaining to collective redundancies and transfers of undertakings (see note 9).

Consultation has to be appropriate with regard to timing, method, and content. It must be with the relevant level of management and on the basis of hard data. Consultation has to be provided in such a way as to enable employees' representatives to meet the employer and obtain a response, and the reasons for that response, to their opinions, and in general undertaken so as to facilitate reaching an agreement.

Member states are to determine the precise procedures to achieve these ends and may limit the information and consultation provisions of the directive to larger undertakings/establishments for some transitional interval. They can also allow the social partners at any appropriate level to negotiate procedures different from those laid down in the legislation provided that they adhere to its general principles. Finally, member states were to provide for adequate sanctions—defined as "effective, proportionate and dissuasive"—to be applicable in the event of infringement of the directive by the employer or the employee side (mainly confidentiality obligations).[15]

8.2.5 Latest Developments

As part of its measures to promote small and medium-size businesses (those with up to 250 employees and a maximum turnover of €50 million), the Commission proposed legislation on a European Private Company in June 2008.[16] The draft legislation is designed to create a common company form that such businesses can use to operate throughput the EU, and thus parallels the ECS. (Indeed, in the case of EPCs formed by mergers the participation requirements are as set down in the ECS directive.) EPCs will be able to transfer their registered offices to another member state. Where such transfer is to a member state with lesser participation rights, special rules apply. In particular, if at least one-third of the EPC's employees are employed in the home member state, negotiations have to take place between management and labor representatives over an agreement on the participation rules that are to apply. Absent agreement, the home country rules serve as the default.

8.3   Raising Rivals' Costs?

Market integration in EU raises the degree of regulatory competition among jurisdictions and may be expected to lower the level of national regulation while encouraging transnational regulation. The latter may be collusive (against internationally mobile capital) or instead seek to raise rivals' costs. Collusion permits governments and powerful interest groups (e.g., labor unions) to maintain a high degree of regulation in the face of market integration: a single country seeking to introduce some measure of employment protection may be expected to lose competitiveness against all other countries whereas if a group of countries can agree on some common labor regulation the loss will be reduced since it is shared among them all (Vaubel, 2008, p. 442). The alternative hypothesis that much of employment/labor legislation in organizations such as the EU can be construed as an attempt to raise rivals' costs implies that members that have a high level of domestic or national regulation are more likely to vote in favor of common or supranational regulations, especially where the latter raise costs in the other countries. Regulatory collusion is predicated on unanimity and the strategy of raising rivals' costs simply on a qualified majority (Vaubel, 2008, p. 447).

Clear examples of regulations that raise rivals costs *within states* have been demonstrated in the literature. Thus, for the United States, cases in point include legislation on minimum wages, regulations under the Federal Occupational Safety and Health Act, and environmental regulations (see the survey in Addison, 2007). For Germany, Vaubel (2007) shows that in the process leading up to and subsequent to German unification in 1871 a Prussian-led majority coalition in the *Bundesrat(h)* imposed their higher trade regulations on the more liberal states in the *Norddeutscher Bund* and in *Baden, Württemberg,* and *Bayern.* A similar process is observed by Feld (2007) for Switzerland in the form of exceptions from freedom of commerce rules for the more conservative, strictly regulated cantons in the interwar period. And in the *supranational context* Boockmann and Vaubel (2005) conclude that voting on International Labor Organization labor standards conforms to the strategy of raising rivals' costs; that is, countries with high labor standards are more prone to vote in favor of common regulations, particularly in those circumstances where these regulations disadvantage other countries by raising their labor costs.

Most recently, Vaubel (2008) has offered a similar interpretation of EU Directives. Given the comparatively small number of labor market directives (31 are identified in the study) that have been openly contested in the 15 years since the voting record of the European Council has been publicly available, his treatment of voting behavior is necessarily informal. Noting that the introduction of qualified majority voting in the EU coincided with measures to strengthen market integration, Vaubel offers several pieces of evidence in support of his contention. First, he considers four directives that were contested in Council. One of these is the 1994 European Works Council (EWC) Directive. As we have seen, the EWC was ultimately processed through the Agreement on Social Policy excluding the British who did not have works councils but including the Portuguese who also did not have them and who like the British were anxious to attract capital (and together with the British confronted the largest increase in the cost of operating multinational councils because of their geographically peripheral position). Portugal duly abstained in the 11-member vote. In each of the other three pieces of contested legislation identified by Vaubel, the British were again in the vanguard of opposition—a position he links to their ranking as the least regulated member state in the Community. Its nearest neighbors in this firmament (Denmark, Ireland, Austria, Finland, the Netherlands, and Sweden) were also among leading opponents of the legislation in question. Vaubel also considers the 2002 directive on national systems for consulting and informing workers, noting that the two chief opponents identified by the distance of their custom and practice from the legislation ultimately voted for the directive realizing that they could not form a blocking minority.

In support of his raising-rivals'-costs argument, Vaubel also offers a review of voting on wider regulatory initiatives in the EU and a brief discussion of differences between European and prior national labor regulations. Each offers tentative support for the model in the form of voting blocs that might carry over to labor regulation and the often large differences in prior national regulations, respectively.

This is an interesting general treatment that suggests why lowering the majority requirements under changes made to the treaties establishing the EU may be expected to stimulate labor regulation. It is also of interest in alerting us to the potential importance of the European dimension in potentially sustaining or undermining national comparative institutional advantages. At issue, however, is the relevance of this portrayal of the conflict between systems to understanding evolving *codetermination issues* in Germany.

8.4 European Legislation from the Perspective of a Multilevel Game. Or, Why German Employers Might Not Seek to Harmonize to a High Level

In an intriguing paper, Callaghan (2003) has criticized the functionalist explanation for the opposition of German and British governments in the Council of Ministers to legal harmonization of worker consultation (and hostile takeovers).[17] The thrust of her argument is that the divergent positions of the two countries is less a question of a "battle between (capitalist) systems" than the result of struggles at the domestic level between and within competing groups. In other words, the standard treatment that governments support rules thought to be vital components of the institutional infrastructures generating the respective comparative institutional advantages of liberal and organized market economies is unsatisfactory because it ignores the political dimension of institutional design that determines actions.

Focusing here on worker consultation, the obvious starting point is that the (ultimate) harmonization sought in the three major pieces of legislation on worker involvement with which we began this chapter is not radical.[18] Why is this? Callaghan would argue that it is the result of less than fundamental divisions between German and British employers. Indeed, she argues that German and British employers have fought against EU-wide imposition of mandatory worker consultation, even if the respective national governments have sought to defend their own domestic arrangements and adopted regime-defensive attitudes.[19]

The debate over worker consultation is said to be subject to centrifugal political tensions within countries, with organized labor and capital pulling in opposite directions. The virtue of Callaghan's treatment is that it identifies the contestation of production regimes from within. Specifically, she identifies and documents four themes of the peak German business federations; respectively, the Confederation of German Employers' Association (*Bundesvereinigung der Deutschen Arbeitgeberverbände*, or BDA) and the Federation of German Industries (*Bundesverband der Deutschen Industrie*, or BDI). First, they have objected to consultation requirements in excess of those obtaining at national level. Second, European initiatives have been viewed as raising the specter of revitalizing codetermination disputes at national level, forcing the employers to cede more ground to the still powerful union movement. Third, on grounds of tissue rejection German *multinationals* were not (initially at least) enamored of the prospect of the exportation of German-style consultation rules to the rest of Europe. Finally, they were committed to a low-consultation model in order to preserve the attractiveness of Germany as a location for foreign investment and of German companies as partners in cross-border mergers.

The crucial bottom line is that it was not German companies that pushed their government to defend the consultation aspect of the German production regime. At root neither they nor superficially less surprisingly their British counterparts favored the spread of consultation requirements. Only the union movement in both countries—albeit in Britain with a distinct lag—supported the spread of consultation requirements and by extension acceptance of the (Franco-)German model.

We think Callaghan's insight that German employers had something to lose from spreading consultation to the rest of Europe even though they are stuck with it in their own country is of crucial historical importance. She reasons that the divergence of practice makes it easier for German employers to resist union demands for a further extension of consultation. We would add the revisionist codicil that promoting ambitious consultation mandates *prevents the German system from adapting.*

8.5 Competition Has Entered the Codetermination Debate

Callaghan's treatment returns us squarely to the contemporary domestic positions taken in the debate over codetermination in Germany. Our starting point is 2004 when the BDA and the BDI set up their own Commission (on codetermination) with the remit of establishing a blueprint for a modernized codetermination, updated to meet specific challenges. It reported in November 2004 (BDA/BDI, 2004). Even without formal institutional change, the Commission argued that the more than 30-year-old German system of *Unternehmensmitbestimmumg* would have to change as a result of globalization of the economy, the increasing international division of labor, the cross-border and cross-national operations of widely dispersed multinationals, EU enlargement, and European developments in company law. Some of the pressures emanating from the latter included the ability of new start-up firms to choose to incorporate as a SE, the codetermination requirements of which were lower than for German public limited companies. Subsidiaries, too, could choose their legal form, so that foreign companies that set up subsidiaries in Germany would not have to follow current German company law in the future. Further, in the case of cross-border mergers and acquisitions, the most extensive type of codetermination that would apply would not be the German variant were it decided to locate the headquarters of the newly merged companies outside the country. (It was also felt in theses circumstances that German companies would not make attractive partners when setting up SEs.)

The BDA/BDI Commission proposed the following changes to company codetermination in the light of these and other challenges.[20] First, it sought negotiated solutions (*Vereinbarungslösungen*) to company codetermination—rather than the one-size-fits-all approach under the 1976 Act—within a framework set by three models for codetermination: quasi-parity codetermination, one-third worker participation, and a consultative council (*Konsultationsrat*) whereby codetermination would be moved outside of the supervisory board. A default or fall-back position of one-third worker representation on the supervisory board was to be reserved for those cases where the parties could not reach agreement—and since unitary or monistic corporate structures are now available in Germany under the ECS Regulation, the BDA/BDI Commission recommmended that the *Konsultationsrat* become the fall-back arrangement in these circumstances. It further recommended that any final agreements on the nature and scope of codetermination be subject to a right of veto on the part of shareholder representatives; specifically, the arrangements would require a three-quarters majority of shareholders. A streamlining of numbers on the supervisory board was also recommended together with allowance for the inclusion of worker representatives from foreign businesses within the group. Finally, the BDA/BDI Commission recommended abolishing the trade unions' legally guaranteed right to supervisory board representation in larger corporations. Instead, all employee representatives—workers and full-time union officials alike—were to be elected by all employees of the company in secret ballot (as under the 1952 Act).

Not surprisingly the union movement rejected the employers' proposals as seeking to narrow the scope of codetermination—and specifically to dismantle (quasi-) parity codetermination in the process—rather than to modernize it (DGB, 2004). The one-third default rule in particular was equated with an attempt to restore "outdated power relations." By way of contrast, the DGB chose to rehearse the standard social arguments in favor of codetermination such as its creating the conditions for the democratic control of economic power and promoting the social acceptability of business. But at the same time it also emphasized the economic advantages of cooperation in facilitating structural change and raising productivity, and the contributions of codetermination in raising investments in human capital investment and reducing transaction costs—citing empirical studies supportive of its case. The broader position of the DGB leadership was that the 1972 Act's threshold of 2,000 employees needed to be reduced substantially (see Sommer, 2006) and indeed that *Montanmitbestimmung* be the yardstick for expanding and developing codetermination.

These diametrically opposing positions foreshadow the "failure" of the tripartite (second) Biedenkopf Commission, appointed by Gerhard Schröder in 2005 to assess the strengths and weaknesses of the German system of codetermination in the light of intensified Europeanization and globalization and propose innovations to the system to ensure its compatibility with the wider European context.[21] Its chairman, Kurt Biedenkopf, announced in November 2006 that the Commission would be unable to issue a joint set of recommendations because of outstanding differences between the employer and employer representatives. As a result, and as noted in chapter 2, the academic members issued their own independent report the following month (Biedenkopf Commission, 2006). They concluded that no fundamental revisions of the existing legislation were in order, while yet recommending some "adaptations" suited to the changed circumstances.

The Biedenkopf Commission's overall assessment of board level representation was favorable. In this assessment it was at pains to emphasize that the goal of the 1976 Act was not economic but rather to provide employees with a democratic voice in company decisions that affected them (consistent with the view of the company as a *social grouping*). Company codetermination was adjudged to have had important social effects (viz. social harmony and social cohesion). As far as the entity's *economic* consequences were concerned, the Commission concluded that the extant econometric evidence (reviewed in chapter 7) was inconclusive on methodological grounds, even if more recent studies were more broadly positive (Biedenkopf Commission, 2006, p. 14). But it felt able to resist the notion that worker directors constituted a source of competitive disadvantage for Germany on the basis of evidence on foreign direct investment, the absence of a codetermination discount in capital markets, and few indications of firms actually avoiding board level representation (p. 18).[22]

Nevertheless, some adaptations were necessary. The change closest to the employers' position was the Commission's recommendation that codetermination rights—degree of involvement, proportion of employee representatives, and overall size of the supervisory board—be negotiated on the basis of an agreement between a negotiating body on the employee side comprising representatives of employees and the union in line with the number of seats each group had on the supervisory board, with decisions being made on a qualified, two-thirds majority.[23]

The other changes recommended by the Biedenkopf Commission were aimed at removing inconsistencies (and complexities) in the existing system of board level representation and governance (e.g., under the current law the management board in private limited-liability companies (*Gesellschaften mit beschränkter Haftung*, GmbHs) has less onerous reporting requirements in relation to the supervisory board than is the case for joint stock companies (*Aktiengesellschaften*, AGs) and the internationalization of company structures (e.g., the need to involve foreign employees employed outside Germany on German supervisory boards). The Commission did not offer any recommendation on the freedom of establishment rule (specifically, in requiring companies incorporated abroad to follow the codetermination practice of their German counterparts).

The SPD-Green coalition government of Gerhard Schröder had committed itself to implementing the recommendations of the Commission and the new CDU/CSU-SPD coalition government of

Chancellor Merkel—sworn in well before Biedenkopf had reported on December 12, 2006—had followed suit, confirming that it would take up the *mutually agreed* recommendations of the Commission and, if necessary, engineer changes to the German system of codetermination (Stettes, 2006). With the publication of a minority report the prospect of any immediate government action is now ruled out. Yet, despite the general acceptance of codetermination as key feature of the social market economy, the challenge resides more in the detail than at any time since 1979.

8.6 Prospects for *Unternehmensmitbestimmung*

The German system of codetermination has been put up for adoption by the market. In that sense it has failed the market test. Board level worker representation on the German pattern has not proved enticing to other nations. To be sure, worker directors are by no means uncommon in Europe (see Carley, 1998; Schulten and Zagelmeyer, 1998), but the practice usually falls well short of the German system. And despite an active European Commission, the attempt to secure harmonization to the German standard has failed. (Note in particular that efforts to model the ECS provisions on worker participation on a German model failed very early on given the strong opposition encountered from liberal market economies.) The stark opposition of German employers to harmonization at a high level has also been important in this connection. To repeat, in all of this we are speaking of *Unternehmensmitbestimmung* rather than *betriebliche Mitbestimmung* since the latter has been rather more successful in influencing (watered-down) European-level mandates seeking to increase the involvement of workers in their companies—even if we have had occasion to note the opposition of German employers to the provisions of the 2001 Works Constitution Act.

Interestingly, our review of the empirical evidence on the economic consequences of worker directors for firm performance in chapter 7 suggested that—subject to potentially very important caveats on the extent of worker representation on company boards (i.e., quasi-parity representation may be excessive) and the presence of union representatives—company codetermination does not seem to have deserved its frankly unenviable international reputation (Addison and Schnabel, 2009). But irrespective of the facts of the case, international events have placed the German system under tremendous strain. We refer to the deliberations of the European Court of Justice, to the passage of the European Company Statute, and the backdrop of a continuing global trend toward the maximization of shareholder wealth as the primary goal of corporate law. These factors are on top of structural problems in the iron, coal, and steel industries, where ongoing company restructuring threatens the continuance of full-parity codetermination.

But the legal changes to which we refer are neither transparent nor settled. Take, for example, the deliberations of the ECJ in the *Centros* case (European Court of Justice, 1999). Here it was decided that a Danish company doing business in Denmark but not in the U.K. could nevertheless incorporate in the U.K. and simultaneously register an office branch in Demark and be subject to British rather than Danish corporate law. This endorsement of freedom of establishment (and seeming contraindication of the so-called real seat theory [*Sitztheorie*], whereby the location of the head office determines which corporate law is applicable) by the ECJ has commonly been interpreted as indicating that Germany will not in these circumstances be able to impose its codetermination system on corporations incorporated in another member state. However, it has recently been argued that the German legislature could legally extend the system of German codetermination to cover pseudo-foreign corporations (under the so-called imperative requirements doctrine—and thus shield the German system from the effects of this incorporation doctrine—even if some aspects of German law would have to change.[24] That said an era of *company law shopping* has begun as evidenced by the fact that as of 2005 every seventh newly established private limited company in Germany was registered according to the legal form of the U.K. (Stettes, 2006; see also Zumbansen, 2002).

Next there is the issue of the European Company Statute (now abstracting from the complications regarding linkage of incorporation and corporate headquarters; on which, see Ringe, 2007). Apart from the additional degree of freedom on incorporation offered by the statute, the more general prospects here are for more flexible codetermination structures anticipated by the Biedenkopf Commmission and demanded by employers, smaller boards tailored to individual company requirements, and new codetermination structures arising from one tier or monistic boards.

The bottom line is that although the issue of convergence has yet to be decided, so that it can still be argued that a European model of corporate governance is implied by the recent initiatives at EU level on EWCs, the ECS, and national systems for informing and consulting workers, changes are afoot. Shareholder value is patently winning ground as an ideology (vis-à-vis stakeholder value). Practical changes are less easy to divine at this stage though we have pointed to new incorporations under U.K. law, the actions of the ECJ (including the Volkswagen case; see Zumbansen and Saam, 2007), and the opportunities opened up by the ECS to indicate that the German system of corporate governance has already changed. At issue are the economic consequences. In the short run, we should at least remain open to the possibility that the differentiated structures that result may be less efficacious than prior institutional complementarities.

CHAPTER 9

Codetermination in Retrospect and Prospect

In this book we have examined the principle of codetermination, reviewed its history, and examined its association with firm performance at the levels of the establishment and the company or enterprise. We also sought to locate the German institution(s) within a European context.

We saw that workplace codetermination or *betriebliche Mitbestimmung* has a long history—at a pinch, almost as long as German democracy itself—although company codetermination or *Unternehmensmitbestimmung* is of altogether more recent vintage having initially been introduced in the coal and steel industries in the immediate postwar period to avert the threat of their being broken up by the occupation authorities. Over the course of time, both types of codetermination have been subject to legislative review. Workplace codetermination has been strengthened, albeit not monotonically, while the reach of company codetermination has been extended beyond the narrow purview of coal, iron, and steel through quasi-parity worker board representation in larger companies (> 2000 employees) and one-third worker board representation in their somewhat smaller counterparts (> 500 employees). More recent changes in the law have tended to reflect the deliberations of tripartite commissions of inquiry into the theory and practice of codetermination. In the process, however, economic criteria have played second fiddle to notions of industrial democracy embedded in the stakeholder model of corporate governance (even if we have been at pains to recognize the existence of supportive economic arguments, devoting one full chapter and part of another to their discussion).

Management has tended to be critical of having to share decision-making power. But it is no exaggeration to say that workplace codetermination has increasingly enjoyed greater acceptance by management, notwithstanding some obvious holdouts such as Lidl, Schlechter, Burger King, and McDonalds and reservations expressed in the debate leading up to the 2001 Works Constitution Act and its aftermath. It is less easy to detect a similar "conversion" in the case of company codetermination. To be sure, the peak *employer* federation (the BDA) has been less confrontational than the peak *industry* confederation, the BDI, in this regard, but it remains a fact that both have found common cause in resisting legal attempts to extend (quasi-) parity codetermination. Such company codetermination continues to be viewed by management as a source of locational disadvantage.

Turning to economic analysis of the impact of codetermination, we identified three phases in the respective research literatures on workplace and company codetermination. (We caution that there is no real empirical investigation of how board representation affects the impact of works councils and vice versa.) Beginning with workplace codetermination, we reported that the early econometric literature was nearly universally hostile to works councils in the sense that their presence was found to be negatively correlated with productivity, profitability, innovation, and (in the case of one study) with lower investment, too. Further, there was no indication that they were even associated with reduced quits. Although there were chinks in the evidence, the overriding impression of this phase of the literature was that works councils were at best constraints that better managers could avoid.

But a variety of statistical lacunae attach to these Phase 1 studies. One major such problem is the issue of their representativeness, stemming from the very small samples of firms investigated (and reinvestigated). The next phase of the literature was able to address this particular problem with the emergence of larger data sets that also allowed other methodological advances. The new literature was to reveal the works council in rather more favorable light—with the major exception of the profitability outcome that is of course by no means an unambiguous performance indicator in the presence of market power, inter alia. Principally, works councils were found to be associated with higher productivity (least controversially in larger plants), reduced labor fluctuation, and even higher employment growth. This literature also provided some support for the theoretical argument that where works councils are embedded in the dual system their pro-productivity potential is most likely to be realized.

Continuing statistical problems meant that this second-stage literature could only be taken so far. Chief among these was the continued reliance upon cross-section data. The next stage of research was able to address this problem, too, although the inertia of the works council entity meant that the solution offered by panel estimation methods was at best partial. The new literature is based on a nationally representative data set, namely, the IAB Establishment Panel. Initially, analyses based on the new data set were to yield even stronger results favoring works councils than the Phase 2 studies. Strangely reminiscent of the early U.S. union-in-the-production-function literature, pro-productive works council effects of around 30 percent were proclaimed. Gradually these were scaled back such that the consensus finding is that productivity effects are likely to be small on average—still a far cry from the first phase literature. And the same would appear to be true of works council effects on other outcome indicators. Thus, in a sharp break with the U.S. union literature, but more in keeping with the broader European evidence in this area, works councils did not appear to impact investment unfavorably. And, abstracting from some lingering controversy concerning the works council role in influencing employment growth and labor turnover, there was also no real suggestion that the entity aggravated the process of employment adjustment (already turgid to begin with in Germany).

If the works council effect on productivity is modest on average, attention then turns on factors that might produce shifts around this average relation. We reported some potentially favorable interactions with training and other high performance work practices, although causality remains an issue because of the unobserved contribution of good management. Finally, some of the earlier optimism emanating from the Phase 2 research *and the theory* was not borne out in Phase 3 studies. Specifically, there is no real indication that if rent seeking is a problem it is mitigated in situations where works council presence coexists with collective bargaining coverage. But, as a practical matter, the new data set has stimulated research into wage determination, even if one would not wish to argue that our understanding of the works council-collective bargaining nexus is other than rudimentary. Some preliminary results are that taken together the two entities may reduce wage dispersion, while works councils may benefit female workers in particular.

Although resting on some of the same arguments as favor works councils, the theoretical case for worker directors from a conventional economics perspective is weaker. Nevertheless, there are some interesting arguments from the agency literature and from oligopolistic competition that serve to buttress the case in favor. Against this has to be set the (very scale of) strident opposition of employers to quasi-parity worker representation on company boards. Interestingly, however, a basic result from this theater of worker participation is that the codetermined company seems to have held up fairly well. As noted above, the research literature on worker directors again conforms to three phases. For its part, the early literature, which has been extensively criticized among other things for its lack of controls, concluded that codetermination (the legislation of 1951, 1952, and 1976) had minimal effects on firm performance. The second phase of research using regression analysis was generally pessimistic, pointing to productivity losses and a sizeable reduction in market-to-book equity ratios in companies with quasi-parity codetermination vis-à-vis those with one-third worker board representation. The consequences of going from one-third to one-half worker representation emerged as most serious in a financial study of 250 stock corporations, using the market-to-book ratio of equity and Tobin's q. (However, in perhaps the most interesting events study of this phase it was reported that employer-friendly and employee-friendly court decisions on codetermination—respectively restricting or extending quasi-parity codetermination—failed to impart any distinctive pattern to cumulative abnormal returns.) Studies of the third phase of research were much more upbeat. First, allowing for firm heterogeneity using panel data, a new study revealed that the deleterious productivity effect of moving to quasi-parity codetermination reported in the second phase of the company codetermination literature was an artifact of cross-section estimation; that is, fixed effects estimation showed no such adverse reaction. Second, a financial study covering *all* publicly held firms traded on the German stock exchange indicated that positive profitability effects could result from *prudent* levels of employee representation in industries requiring more intense coordination and information sharing—indicating that monitoring by worker directors could reduce shirking behavior among managers—while suggesting that the negative findings of the key financial study of the second phase reflected sample size considerations, the partial neglect of agency considerations, and the fact that union representatives were more likely to be encountered on company boards in this particular sample. Finally, although the material is sparse, other recent studies have pointed to not unfavorable profitability and R&D outcomes in codetermined companies.

The bottom lines, therefore, are that works councils have gradually received more support from an evolving literature (even if claims of a productivity differential of 30 percent should be strongly resisted) while outside of *Montanmitbestimmung* firms with quasi-parity codetermination may well have held their own to date (despite widespread dissatisfaction among employer groups with the worker director model). But, as we have also seen, works councils are in modest if not precipitous decline while there is no support for the German worker director model as a template for social policy in the European Union.

What then are the prospects for codetermination in Germany? At the level of works councils, it would be both premature and wrong to predict their demise. There is still more than a measure of support for the famous words of Berthold Beitz to the effect that if works councils didn't exist they would have to be invented. Assuredly, no one has proposed the dismantling of workplace codetermination. To the contrary it has served as a template for EU policies seeking to increase the involvement of workers in their companies and recent changes in domestic law have sought to strengthen works councils and to increase the likelihood of their election. Although the new Works Constitution Act has revived some of the old employer misgivings about works council excesses—for example, their acting "contrary to their duties"—their place seems to us assured. However, works councils have been in decline for some years now and there is no sign that changes in the law have stimulated their formation. This has of course led to the claim that there is a codetermination gap or deficit in Germany. At a descriptive level this seems to be borne out by the evidence, but it does not follow that there is a participation deficit in Germany or that the future will represent a continuation of the past in this regard. On the former question, there are other channels of employee involvement including teamwork and formal bodies other than works councils. At issue are whether teamwork and other high performance work practices are alternatives or substitutes for works councils and whether the bodies analogous to works councils have materially different economic effects (though it should not go unsaid that we need to know much more of the operation of works councils themselves). On the latter question, the future of works councils is also tied in with wider developments in corporate governance. Thus, for example, the role of works councils will expand as part of the negotiating process over precise forms of worker participation that is central to the formation of European Companies.

The future of codetermination at company level is much more difficult to divine, and debate over its future is much more divisive. Even though company codetermination has held up remarkably well and as far as we have been able to determine has seemingly not had economic effects of a magnitude that would lead to its abandonment (or, to be fair, its adoption by the market), the fact remains that it is unpopular among German employers and viewed with suspicion from outside the country. Perceptions are not unimportant of course in shaping the future and we feel that the possibility to establish alternative forms of corporate governance without quasi-parity codetermination under changes in company law and the passage of the European Company Statute do portend material changes in the future, despite inbuilt inertia (e.g., the "before and after principle" in the case of the SE). Although there is little as yet to suggest an "escape" from codetermination, we feel that an erosion of the quasi-parity model is implied, perhaps with a one-third representation model as a default. There is even the prospect of convergence toward an Anglo-Saxon model with the profound export orientation of the German economy. This is an altogether more controversial prognosis, however, and any tendency in this direction likely to have been diverted or postponed by the current financial crisis. But, to repeat, the role of the works council is likely to expand, because its future may be underwritten both by experimentation with and movement away from quasi-parity codetermination.

Notes

2 Context: What Is Codetermination?

1. For a fuller discussion of the varieties-of-capitalism approach—essentially the distinction between the Anglo-Saxon liberal market economy typified by the United States and the coordinated market economies such as Germany (and France)—that argues that the institutions of capitalism differ from country to country by reason of strong institutional complementarities, see Michel Albert (1993) and Hall and Soskice (2001). An equivalent distinction is that between the "shareholder" and "stakeholder" models of corporate governance (see Rebérioux, 2002).

2. Its antecedents are even earlier in the form of a draft Industrial Code discussed in Constituent National Assembly in 1848 that sought the establishment of factory committees with legal participation rights.

3. We abstract from two other pieces of legislation enacted in the interstices. The first is the 1974 Federal Staff Representation Act (or *Personalvertretungsgesetz*) that expanded codetermination at establishment level in the public sector (initiated in 1955 and amended in 1965). The second is the Executives' Committee Act (*Sprecherausschussgesetz*) of 1988 that set up executive councils for senior executives, and also made provision for a modest extension of information and consultation rights for works councils proper in the event of changes in technology.

4. The streamlined procedure has two stages: the nomination of candidates by an electoral board (*Wahlvorstand*), followed one week later by another works meeting (*Betriebsversammlung*) in which the works council is elected directly in a secret ballot of all employees present.

5. As does the Works Constitution Act, the Codetermination Act exempts companies with political, trade union, religious, charitable, educational, or artistic goals.

6. The election procedure for employee representatives is complicated and varies by type of company and type of codetermination. In the case of full-parity codetermination (and abstracting from the Supplementary Codetermination Act of 1956) the size of the supervisory board is determined by share capital. Let us assume that the supervisory board has 21 members. In this case, eight

members each are appointed by shareholders and the employees. Each side has two additional members that are not affiliated with the company. Four of the employee representatives must be employees of the company and are nominated by the works council and the remaining employee representatives and the additional members are proposed by the central bodies of unions represented in the plant. (An agreement between shareholders and employees has to be reached on the neutral member.) The works councilors appoint all employee representatives and the other members on the employee side. The candidates appointed by the unions have also to be confirmed by the works council. In each case confirmation by the meeting of shareholders is a formality.

Under the 1952 Act, as amended in 2004 (under the Third Part Act or *Drittelbeteiligungsgesetz*), the size of the supervisory board again depends on share capital and comprises a minimum of 3 and a maximum of 21 members (intermediate sizes must be divisible by 3). If there are only one or two employee members these must work in the company. If there are three of more employee representatives, external persons such as trade union representatives may be appointed by the employees. The supervisory board members are elected directly by the employees. The works council and one-tenth or 100 of the employees of the company may propose candidates.

Finally, under the 1976 Act supervisory boards have the same number of shareholder and employee representatives. Their overall size is now a function of employment in the company: 12 members up to 10,000 employees, 16 members up to 20,000 employees, and 20 members thereafter. Trade union representation is guaranteed: the unions have 2 seats where the supervisory board has 12 or 16 members and 3 seats where there are more than 20 members. The other seats of the employee representatives (alternately, 4, 6, or 7) are reserved for employees of the company. In principle, in companies with up to 8,000 more employees, the election of employee members is direct whereas it is by delegates when the company has more than 8,000 employees. In practice, employees can opt for either of the election methods. The employee representatives must include at least one wage earner, one salaried employee, and one managerial employee. Managerial staff representatives have to be nominated by 5 percent of managerial staff, or 20 such employees. For white- and blue-collar employees the corresponding values are one-fifth or 100 such employees. Overall, in the 729 companies with more than 2,000 employees there are some 5,142 employee representatives, including some 1,700 union officials. There are around 2,000 companies with one-third employee representation.

7. Note that this inquiry might be termed *Biedenkopf Zwei* since Kurt Biedenkopf had first been commissioned by the government to evaluate worker board level representation some 25 years earlier. His report culminated in the 1976 Codetermination Act; see Biedenkopf Commission (1970).

8. The preoccupations of the 1998 *Kommission Mitbestimmung*, discussed earlier, were with the system of codetermination as a whole. Thus, it favored a holistic approach based on the maintenance of a division of tasks between codetermination and collective bargaining. It also viewed the use of codetermination as part of a controlled decentralization of the collective bargaining system.

9. Other union preoccupations included the lack of defined management board activities that required the agreement of the supervisory board, and the failure of the Commission to elevate the powers of the Labor Director (while making his or her appointment contingent on the agreement of the worker side) or to consider lowering the employment size threshold at which parity representation was activated.

10. Again, the following discussion focuses on the 2001 Works Constitution Act and hence to works councils and not to "staff councils" (*Personalräte*) in the public sector. A full English translation of the legislation is available at http://www.bmwi.de/English/Redaktion/Pdf/__Archiv/labour-law/works-constitution-act1,property=pdf,bereich=bmwi,sprache=de,rwb=true.pdf

11. All employees can vote from the age of 18 years, but only those who have worked for the firm for at least 6 months are eligible.

12. The central works council (*Gesamtbetriebsrat*) is found where there are several works councils in one company. It comprises the members of the individual works councils. Its competence is limited to matters that affect several plant councils that cannot be settled in-house. The group works council (*Konzernbetriebsrat*) is found in groups of companies and is not automatic. Its authority is limited to matters impacting the concern as a whole or a subset of its subsidiaries.

13. The overall membership of the works council varies according to the number of employees with voting rights normally employed in the establishment. It ranges from 1 member where there are 5–20 such employees through to 35 members where there are 7,001–9,000 employees. Thereafter, the size of the council increases by 2 members for each incremental 3,000 employees.

14. These general duties include the right of supervision, namely, to see that effect is given to Acts, ordinances, safety regulations, collective agreements, and works agreements for the benefit of employees (§ 80 (1) WCA), and the right to make recommendations (§ 80 (2) WCA).

15. And in establishments with more than 300 employees, the works council may retain a consultant to support it.

16. On ad hoc and permanent conciliation committees, their composition, structure, and decision making, see §§ 76 (1) through (8) WCA.

17. In establishments with more than 500 employees the works council may request the drawing up of guidelines (i.e., a right to initiate) on the technical, personal, and social criteria to be applied in the planning of employee recruitment, transfer, regrading, and dismissal measures (§ 95 (2) WCA).

18. The existing pattern of works council frequency seems to be fairly well explained by strucutral/organizational variables and elements associated with the specific functions of the works council; see, for example, Addison, Schnabel, and Wagner, 1997; Hübler and Jirjahn, 2003.
19. Begründung zum Entwurf eines Gesetzes zur Reform des Betriebsverfassungsgesetzes (Referentenentwurf), p. 23.
20. Deutscher Bundestag, 14. Wahlperiode, Drucksache 14/5741 of 2. 4. 2001, p. 32.

3 The Theory of Codetermination

1. We should also note that in discussing monitoring and auditing procedures subsequent developments of the idiosyncratic exchange variant of contract theory do reserve a specific role for unions; see Riordan and Wachter (1983).
2. More recently, the unions-as-a-commitment-device has also been extended to cover the financing of general training investments; see, for example, Dustmann and Schönberg (2004).
3. We will not dwell on the dissatisfaction stimulus that drives behavior in both the product and labor market models, since in according "institutional response" equal billing in the model (see below) the architects of collective voice clearly regard good union-management relations as central to performance outcomes.
4. As Freeman and Medoff (1984, p. 165) state, "Some managements will adjust to the union and turn unionism into a positive force at the workplace; others will not. Over the long run, those that respond positively will prosper while those that do not will suffer in the market place."
5. For both of the above public goods arguments to have force, there must be costs to the use of external markets (since if quitting were costless the individual worker could simply choose upfront the employer whose working conditions most closely approximated his or her own preferences) and the workplace must continue to be buffeted by unforeseen shocks (otherwise, there would be no need for the union's demand-revealing function after the initial match between employer and employee) (Freeman, 1976).
6. Freeman (1976, p. 365) also observes that in larger organizations union voice will also provide central management with information about local conditions and operations of a type that differs markedly from that passed up through the organizational chain (the theory of teams).
7. Lower profits are found irrespective of the profit measure, whether it be the price-cost margin, an accounting measure (e.g., the rate of return on sales or capital), or a market value measure (such as Tobin's q). This result also obtains irrespective of type of study, including events analyses involving changes in market value associated with union representation elections or unanticipated changes in collective bargaining.

8. In discussing this solution to postcontractual information asymmetry, Freeman and Lazear also illustrate how a voluntary codetermination arrangement might not arise. To this end, they now assume that there are two types of employee, one of which is always prepared to make concessions while the other will only do so following legitimization of the relevant information by a worker representative body. For its part, the employer cannot distinguish between the two types. In these circumstances, a mandate might improve the situation by avoiding bankruptcy when the employer judges employees incorrectly.

9. Freeman and Lazear (1995, p. 48) are actually more explicit in addressing *German* codetermination in the context of its ability to enhance job security which the authors view as crucial in bringing worker interests more in line with those of shareholders.

10. Author's translation of a question contained in the German IAB Establishment Panel. Research into these works council-like bodies and their impact is in its infancy (e.g., Ellguth, 2005).

11. This is the so-called free riding or $1/n$ problem, where n is the number of employees. The tendency for the individual to shirk can be reduced by horizontal monitoring, namely, by employee monitoring of their co-workers.

12. Group rather than individual because the regimes we are discussing are likely to be characterized by interdependent and overlapping tasks and employee decision-making autonomy.

13. Indeed, the latter might be construed as piercing the veil shrouding the black box of collective voice productivity-increasing mechanisms.

14. Freeman and Lazear (1995) are an honorable exception to this statement. They show that the specific rules for selecting works councils will affect their representativeness and also that workers with minority view are likely to run for office raising the possibility of "maverick" councils dominated by small cliques. See also Gallego (2007).

15. For an interesting early U.S. study of the agency problem in which the lower monitoring costs of the union (than the principal) lead to higher managerial effort and higher measured labor productivity, see Kuhn, 1985.

4 The Early Econometric Literature on Works Councils

1. Table 4.1 draws on Addison, Schnabel, and Wagner (2004, Table 1, pp. 258–259). The main difference is the addition of the a new study in row 8. Minor changes have also been made to three other row entries.

2. In addition to this direct effect, the authors argue that a more highly unionized workforce is more likely to elect a council.

3. FitzRoy and Kraft (1985, p. 550) attribute the insignificance of the works council dummy in their wage equation to two offsetting tendencies: first, management may raise wages to preempt the formation of a works council;

second, however, works councils have some bargaining power that can increase wages.

4. Most firms did not gather detailed information on quits because of the generally favorable turnover situation; for example, just 14 percent of the sample claimed to have high quit rates among skilled workers.

5. For example, wages and training expenditures had a negative impact on quits and flow production a positive effect; and quit rates were found to be higher the more closely workers were supervised.

6. For a discussion transcending the economic boundaries, the reader is referred to the interesting studies of Wever (1994) and Frege (2002) and the references contained therein.

7. For example, slowed employment growth attendant upon an attempt to recast outmoded workplace organization into a form more amenable to technical change, or the abandonment of restrictive work practices, might give the appearance of inferior performance, while padded employment achieved by job guarantees (an aspect of rent seeking) might alternatively be construed as indicating a good performance.

5 The Emergence of a More Positive View of Workplace Codetermination: Evidence from Some Larger Datasets

1. The earliest and best-known classification system is that of Kotthoff (1994).

2. The industrial relations reality is of course that there is also collective bargaining at firm level. The role of firm level agreements and their interaction with works councils is only now beginning to be exploited in the literature and is only touched upon in what follows.

3. Say, by withholding consent in areas where it has codetermination rights.

4. Since this application seems to hinge on bargaining external to the firm, a real issue is raised by the growing tendency toward company level collective agreements. The number of German firms bargaining at the company level has increased since 1990. There is no analysis of this development in this phase of German research. For the future it would be interesting to see—in the manner of the earlier Phase 1 literature—whether the effects on workplace economic performance are differentiated when both the union and the works council are active at the company level.

5. By the same token, it will be recalled that among firms that did not practice profit sharing FitzRoy and Kraft confirm their earlier finding of a negative and statistically significant association between works council presence and productivity.

6. Table 5.1 draws on Addison, Schbnabel, and Wagner (2004, Table 2, pp. 264–267) but adds information on the first quantile-regression study of

productivity as well as a summary of findings from a very recent analysis of employment change.

7. Slightly larger absolute effects are reported by Frick (1996): reductions of 3.2 percentage points in the case of dismissals and 3.2 percentage points in the case of quits, again over a two-year interval.

8. But note that quits cannot be separately identified in the Hanover Firm Panel because they are embedded in a composite measure of departures or separations that includes dismissals, retirements, and deaths. The same is true of the NIFA "departures" measure.

9. Pending that discussion, we should also point out that controversy attaches to some of the quit estimates. In particular, Kraft (2006) has recently reported that he was unable to replicate Frick's (1996) using the same Büchtemann-Höland data set.

10. Elsewhere one of these authors reports that, among firms with 21–100 employees, wages are higher in works council establishments irrespective of whether or not the plant is covered by a collective agreement; see Jirjahn (2003a).

11. Although we should note that this is the case only for the full sample; among smaller plants with 21–100 employees this is not the case.

12. Other innovations introduced in the final phase of research identified in chapter 7 include the analysis of survival bias and the deployment of dynamic labor adjustment models that also allow one to recoup the employment change effect.

13. Although studies of *labor fluctuation* often point to a reduction of hires in works council settings, this result is not universal; for example, Frick (1996, 1997) suggests that works councils have a positive effect on hires in *growing* firms. Moreover, where works councils are found to reduce labor fluctuation (i.e., the sum of hires plus separations), there are also indications of increased adjustment along other margins; for example, Dilger (2002) reports that works councils are positively associated with the use of flextime. Finally, there are no indications in this literature that works councils hinder reductions in force in contracting firms (Frick, 1996).

14. Abstracting from the issue of the works council-collective bargaining nexus, the main point is that although several studies find evidence of higher wages in works council regimes (e.g., Meyer, 1995a, 2001), the source of these higher earnings is not transparent. For example, in investigating the gap between the wage fixed at industry/regional level and that paid at the establishment, Addison, Schnabel, and Wagner's (2001) OLS estimates fail to reveal any *general* indication of works council influence (see row 2 of table 5.1). That said, these authors are able to identify situations in which management chooses to discuss or negotiate supplementary payments with the works council and it is precisely in these circumstances that a statistically significant positive association between works council and wage gap emerges.

6 The Impact of Workplace Codetermination: Findings from the Third Phase of Research

1. There have been 17 industries since 2004. Between 2000 and 2003 there were 20 industries and 16 industries prior to that.
2. Further examples include the recruitment of skilled workers, the hiring of older workers, and measures to assist the employment of older workers and to improve work-life balance.
3. Value-added is obtained from the survey respondent's estimate of the percentage share of total sales represented by materials cost. Accordingly, 1 minus this share is then used in conjunction with sales volume to derive value added. Unfortunately, in addition to the missing values problem, there is every indication of measurement error: Addison, Schank, Schnabel, and Wagner (2006) point out that almost two-thirds of the observations are in multiples of 5 percent, while the reported share of materials changes on average by almost 12 percent in any two years, which is adjudged unrealistically high for the sample periods in question.
4. Although as we shall see, training investments have been the subject of greater scrutiny.
5. These findings differ materially from those reported in the Anglo-Saxon union literature but less fundamentally from two comparatively recent German cross-section studies not cited in the table. Hübler (2003) reports that works council presence is associated with higher levels of ICT investment, other investment, and expansion investment. Set in a three-equation model, this positive overall effect is found to stem exclusively from the indirect effects of works councils operating through reorganization and training. For its part, the direct effect of works councils on investment is negative although not statistically significant. In a companion study by Gerlach, Hübler, and Meyer (2002), using three years of IAB data, this inverse association is statistically significant in one specification. But, to repeat, these studies rely on single cross-sections of data and only make use of information on works council presence (rather than changes in works council status), with the result that any attribution of causality is difficult.
6. But interpretation is not altogether transparent. If it is shown that, other things being equal, works councils raise wages (see below), then employment growth should be depressed. If workplace representation keeps the level of employment too high—another form of rent seeking—then this too will adversely impact growth. Equally, works councils may make firms more reluctant to hire labor because of the subsequent difficulty of shedding it because of the web of job security provisions and severance packages/social plans (see below). The effects of worker representation on investment may also play a role, although we have tended to discount this particular explanation in the light of recent German research. If all of these factors do predispose us to expect a negative effect of workplace

representation on employment it does not necessarily follow that reduced employment is a bad thing if experienced in conjunction with organizational change and a shakeout of restrictive/protective employment practices.

7. See the studies by Frick (2001) and Dilger (2002) in rows 6 and 7 of table 5.1. See also the discussion of FitzRoy and Kraft (1995) in chapter 4.

8. The same is true of the *union*-EI/HPWP nexus. Key U.S. studies examining this interaction are Cooke (1994) and Black and Lynch (2001, 2004); see the discussion in Addison (2005).

9. In addition to using the within estimator to derive average residuals for each establishment, the authors also use a GMM estimator *in the first step* to deal with biases stemming from the endogeneity of capital, labor, and materials.

10. Most of the other training coefficients increase as well.

11. For an intriguing German language study of the links between investment, further training, and reorganization, see Gerlach, Hübler, and Meyer (2002).

12. Earlier research looking into the wage gap either reports no works council effect or even detects a negative influence (see, respectively, Meyer 1995a; Bellmann and Kohaut, 1995).

13. Hübler and Jirjahn (2003) argue that it is in the interests of both the employer side at industry/regional level *and* the union side to prevent works councils from rent seeking.

14. In the only study using the Hanover Firm Panel to investigate skill differentials, Hübler and Meyer (2001) examine the determinants of differences between the highest effective wages of skilled and unskilled workers. Both industrial relations entities are instrumented as in Hübler and Jirjahn (2003). The authors' OLS estimates suggest that works councils reduce and collective agreements increase the wage spread.

15. For more information on bargaining coverage and the wage structure, see Gerlach and Stephan (2006). See also the references in Fitzenberger, Kohn, and Lembcke (2008), pp. 10–11.

16. In an earlier paper, using IAB data for 1995–2002, Gürtzgen (2004) reports that (average) wages are less responsive to rents (again, as measured by the difference between annual sales, material costs, and the alternative wage) under collective agreements than in their absence. Indeed, in her dynamic estimates wages in covered establishments appear insensitive to rents, suggesting that there are unobserved plant characteristics in covered establishments that are associated with both higher profits and higher wages. She speculates that a compressed intrafirm wage structure under collective bargaining causes firms to hire better quality workers. Although works councils are included as a regressor in this study, they are not interacted with rents and their effect on wages is positive and well determined only in the pooled OLS estimates.

17. Also, since wage compression is also involved, unions facilitate firm-financed general training in this model. See also Acemoglu and Pischke (1999).

7 Codetermination at the Enterprise Level

1. We should perhaps go back earlier, since the base legislation (i.e., full-parity codetermination) is often depicted as having been forced on the nation after the 1939–1945 war by the British inter alia as punishment of the iron and steel barons for their support of the NSDAP regime (Streeck, 1992).

2. The ideology of social inclusion and cooperation is of course the other explanation for the establishment of codetermination. On the vexed question of whether industrial peace is good for the economy, see the cross-country analysis of Addison and Teixeira (2009).

3. Kraft (2001) tests his model by focusing on the determinants of the price-cost margin in 22 German firms, 1972–1994. Evidence compatible with codetermined firms evincing different behavior is obtained.

4. Note that the omitted category consists of publicly quoted companies (because of the need to obtain financial information) but since these are necessarily noncodetermined they are not typical of the firmament of publicly quoted companies.

5. It is 28 rather than 23 because in one case 6 companies lodged a joint appeal to the Federal Constitutional Court.

6. When one-third representation is compared with almost-equal representation, the stock market premium is correspondingly higher, in the range 38–67 percent.

7. But we should note that Gorton and Schmid (2004, p. 89) caution that "codetermination-induced productivity effects cannot be ruled out."

8. Data from the late 1970s were dropped because of possible transition effects during that time frame.

9. Although, as the author admits, the implied growth in productivity and profits—at 16.8 percent and DM 60.5 million, respectively—seem "pretty high intuitively" (Renaud, 2007, fn. 22).

10. For an interesting German language study using data for 2002 and 2003 that links significantly *negative* employment effects to trade union representation on company boards, see Werner and Zimmermann (2005).

11. Logit results are also provided for dividend payouts (circumstances where the firm pays a dividend = 1, 0 otherwise). Firms are significantly more likely to pay dividends when there are employee representatives on the board and the interaction of employee representation with the operating income to sales ratio is also positive, which the authors take to suggest that labor facilitates the payment of a cash dividend and mitigates appropriation by insiders and large shareholders. In short, employee representatives

bring to the table a knowledge base that complements that of shareholder representatives.

12. Although the union side has proven adept in marshalling evidence and in presenting its case; see, for example, Vitols (2006).

8 European Rules for Informing and Consulting Employees and the European Dimension

1. See, respectively, "Council Directive 75/129/EEC of 17 February 1975 on the approximation of the laws of the Member States relating to collective redundancies." *Official Journal of the European Communities* L 48 of 22.2.1975; "Council Directive of 14 February 1977 on the approximation of the laws of the Member States relating to the safeguarding of employees' rights in the event of transfers of undertakings, businesses, or parts of businesses, 77/187/EEC." *Official Journal of the European Communities* L 161 of 5.3.1977; "Council Directive of 20 October 1980 on the approximation of the laws of the Member States relating to the protection of employees in the event of the insolvency of their employer, 80/987/EEC." *Official Journal of the European Communities* L 283 of 28.10.80.

2. See, respectively, "Proposal for a Council Directive on procedures for informing and consulting employees of undertakings with complex structures, in particular transnational undertakings." COM(80) 243 final. Brussels: Commission of the European Communities, 1980; "Amended proposal for a Council Directive on procedures for informing and consulting employees." COM(83) 292 final. Brussels: Commission of the European Communities, 1983.

3. "Proposal for a Council Regulation embodying a statute for a European Company." *Official Journal of the European Communities* C 124 of 10.10.1970.

4. See, respectively, "Proposal for a Fifth Directive to coordinate the safeguards which, for the protection of the interests of members and others, are required by Member States of companies within the meaning of the second paragraph of Article 58 of the EEC Treaty, as regards the structure of sociétés anonymes and the powers and obligations of their organs." *Official Journal of the European Communities* C 7 of 28.1.1972; "Amended Proposal for a Fifth Directive founded on Article 54 (3)(g) of the EEC treaty concerning the structure of public limited companies and the powers and obligations of their organs." *Official Journal of the European Communities* C 240 of 9.9.1983.

5. During the 1991 intergovernmental negotiations leading up to the revision of the treaties establishing the common market, the Commission sought to extend the reach of social policy and to widen the treaty basis permitting qualified majority voting beyond the tenuous hold of Article 118A. To this end it proposed a special *social chapter* to the new treaty—the Treaty on

European Union, or Maastricht Treaty as it is more popularly known. The opposition of the U.K. meant that a political compromise was necessary to save the wider treaty. The formula was to relegate the terms of what would have been the social chapter to a *Protocol on Social Policy* appended to the Treaty on European Union of 1991. Annexed to the Protocol was an *Agreement on Social Policy*. The Protocol was signed by all (of the then) 12 member states and noted the intention of 11 of their number to use the machinery of the Community to implement an *Agreement on Social Policy* that specifically excluded the U.K.

6. Consisting at that time of the Union of Industrial and Employers' Confederations of Europe (UNICE), subsequently renamed BusinessEurope/ the Confederation of European Business in 2007, the European Centre of Enterprises with Public Participation (CEEP), and the European Trade Union Confederation (ETUC).

7. Council Directive 94/45/EC of 22 September 1994 on the establishment of a European Works Council or a procedure in Community-scale undertakings and Community-scale groups of undertakings for the purposes of informing and consulting employees." *Official Journal of the European Communities* OJ L 254 of 30.9.1994.

8. "Proposal for a Directive of the European Parliament and Council on the establishment of a European Works Council or a procedure in Community-scale undertakings and Community-scale groups of undertakings for the purposes of informing and consulting employees (recast)." COM(2008) 419. Brussels: Commission of the European Communities, 2008.

9. See, respectively, "Council Directive 98/59/EC of 20 July 1998 on the approximation of the laws of the Member States relating to collective redundancies." *Official Journal of the European Communities* L 225 of 12.8.1998; "Council Directive 2001/23/EC of 12 March 2001 on the approximation of the laws of the Member States relating to the safeguarding of employees' rights in the event of transfers of undertakings, businesses or parts of undertakings or businesses." *Official Journal of the European Communities* L 82 of 22.3.2001.

10. A single company based in the EU may transform itself into an SE if for at least two years it has had a subsidiary governed by the laws of anther member state.

11. The savings in administration and legal cost are estimated to amount to between €30 and €35 billion a year (Rebérioux, 2002, p. 127).

12. See, respectively, "Council Regulation (EC) No. 2157/2001 of 8 October 2001 on the Statute for a European Company (SE)." *Official Journal of the European Communities* L 294 of 10.11.2001; "Council Directive 2001/86/ EC of 8 October 2001 supplementing the Statute for a European company with regard to the involvement of employees." *Official Journal of the European Communities* L 80 of 10.11.2001.

13. In this case, an SE formed via merger and *a priori* concerned with this reference rule could not register in this member state.

14. "Directive 2002/14/EC of the European Parliament and of the Council of 11 March 2002 establishing a general framework for informing and consulting employees in the European Community." *Official Journal of the European Communities* L 80 of 23.3.2002.

15. Notwithstanding the British opt-out, future Community policy on informing and consulting workers may be expected to draw on the so-called Charter of Fundamental Rights of the European Union (*Official Journal of the European Communities* C364/1 of 18.12.2000), now incorporated into the Reform Treaty. In particular, the fourth *chapter* of the Charter, which covers inter alia worker rights to timely information and consultation (Article 27), presages scope for the extension of social policy in this area at the hands of the ECJ.

16. "Proposal for a Council Regulation on the Statute for a European private company." COM(2008) 396/3. Brussels: Commission of the European Communities.

17. See also Callaghan (2007, 2008).

18. That said, the possibility that the Commission will carefully pick its time to revisit the legislation with a view to stiffening their terms cannot be ruled out; after all, that is what the history of the considerable majority of its initiatives suggests (Addison and Siebert, 1994).

19. Even if on the issue of takeover legislation the employers have pulled in opposite directions, the result of which according to Callaghan (2003, p. 4) has merely been to create the appearance of a battle of the systems.

20. That said, roughly one-fifth of its report was given over to works councils of which the peak employer confederations were also critical. In particular, it was argued that the 2001 reform of the Works Constitution Act (see chapter 2) had made workplace codetermination more bureaucratic and cumbersome and hence more expensive to operate. The Commission therefore sought a reduction in the number of full-time works councilors. It also sought an increase in the legal threshold of the number of employees required to establish a works council, and recommended that a works council should only be set up if at least one-third of employees entitled to vote in the election actually participated in it. At the same time, the Commission looked to a decentralization of collective bargaining by ceding a greater negotiating role to the works council at the expense of trade unions, while at the same time seeking a reduction in the range of issues over which works councils had codetermination rights.

21. Recall that the first Biedenkopf Commission (1970), which reported in 1970, ultimately led to quasi-parity board representation under the 1976 Codetermination Act

22. And for the Commission's interpretation of a survey of management attitudes to codetermination and its assessment of two McKinsey surveys on confidence in national systems of corporate control, see Biedenkopf Commission (2006, p. 16 and p. 18, respectively).

23. We commented earlier on the fact that the negotiations were not to be led by the union and that under certain conditions the union might have no direct role at board level. Necessarily this recommendation much exercised the union movement. By the same token, the employer side was dissatisfied with the Commission's favorable assessment of company codetermination, the possibility of a bargained *increase* in worker representation from one-third to one-half of the supervisory board, and the Commission's insistence that in the event of failure to agree the 1976 Act would remain the default for companies with more than 2,000 employees.

24. In particular, the German law on full-parity codetermination could not be extended to pseudo-foreign companies and certain loopholes in the German law concerning controlling agreements and limited partnerships would have to be excised (Dammann, 2003).

Bibliography

Acemoglu, Daron and Jörn-Steffen Pischke. 1999. "The Structure of Wages and Investment in General Training." *Journal of Political Economy* 107 (June): 539–572.

Addison, John T. 2005. "The Determinants of Firm Performance: Unions, Works Councils, and Employee Involvement/High Performance Work Practices." *Scottish Journal of Political Economy* 52 (July): 406–450.

———. 2007. "Politico-Economic Causes of Labor Regulation in the United States—Rent Seeking, Alliances, Raising Rivals' Costs (Even Lowering One's Own?) and Interjurisdictional Competition." In Peter Bernholz and Roland Vaubel (eds.), *Political Competition and Economic Regulation*. London and New York: Routledge, pp. 19–42.

———. 2008. "In the Beginning There Was Social Policy: Developments in Social Policy in the European Union from 1972 through 2008." Unpublished Paper. University of South Carolina.

Addison, John T., Lutz Bellmann, and Arndt Kölling. 2004. "Works Councils and Plant Closings in Germany." *British Journal of Industrial Relations* 42 (March): 125–148.

Addison, John T., Lutz Bellmann, Claus Schnabel, and Joachim Wagner. 2004. "The Reform of the German Works Constitution Act: A Critical Appraisal." *Industrial Relations* 43 (April): 392–420.

Addison, John T., Kornelius Kraft, and Joachim Wagner. 1993. "German Works Councils and Firm Performance." In Bruce E. Kaufman and Morris M. Kleiner (eds.), *Employee Representation: Alternatives and Future Directions*. Madison, WI: Industrial Relations Research Association, pp. 305–308.

Addison, John T., Thorsten Schank, Claus Schnabel, and Joachim Wagner. 2006. "Works Councils in the Production Process." *Schmollers Jahrbuch* 126 (2): 251–283.

———. 2007. "Do Works Councils Inhibit Investment?" *Industrial and Labor Relations Review* 60 (January): 187–203.

Addison, John T. and Claus Schnabel. 2009. "Worker Directors: A German Product that Didn't Export?" IZA Discussion Paper No. 3918. Bonn: Institut zur Zukunft der Arbeit/Institute for the Study of Labor.

Addison, John T., Claus Schnabel, and Joachim Wagner. 1996. "German Works Councils, Profits and Innovation." *Kyklos* 49 (4): 555–582.

Addison, John T., Claus Schnabel, and Joachim Wagner. 1997. "On the Determinants of Mandatory Works Councils in Germany." *Industrial Relations* 36 (October): 419–445.

———. 1998. "Betriebsräte in der deutschen Industrie: Verbreitung, Bestimmungsgründe und Effekte." In Knut Gerlach, Olaf Hübler, and Wolfgang Meyer (eds.), *Ökonomische Analysen betrieblicher Strukturen und Entwicklungen—Das Hannoveraner Firmenpanel.* Frankfurt: Campus Verlag, pp. 59–86.

———. 2000a. "Nonunion Representation in Germany." In Bruce E. Kaufman and Daphne Gottlieb Taras (eds.), *Nonunion Employee Representation—History, Contemporary Practice, and Policy.* Armonk, NY: M.E. Sharpe, pp. 365–385.

———. 2000b. "Die mitbestimmungsfreie Zone aus ökonomischer Sicht." *Hamburger Jahrbuch für Wirtschafts-und Gesellschaftspolitik* 45, pp. 277–292.

———. 2000c. "Die mitbestimmungsfreie Zone—eine Problemfeld?" *Wirtschaftsdienst* 6 (June): 361–365.

———. 2001. "Works Councils in Germany: Their Effects on Establishment Performance." *Oxford Economic Papers* 53 (October): 659–694.

———. 2004. "The Course of Research into the Economic Consequences of German Works Councils." *British Journal of Industrial Relations* 42 (June): 255–281.

Addison, John T. and W. Stanley Siebert. 1991. "The Social Charter of the European Community: Evolution and Controversies." *Industrial and Labor Relations Review* 44 (July): 597–625.

———. 1994. "Recent Developments in Social Policy in the New European Union." *Industrial and Labor Relations Review* 48 (October): 5–27.

Addison, John T., W. Stanley Siebert, Joachim Wagner, and Xiangdong Wei. 2000. "Worker Participation and Firm Performance." *British Journal of Industrial Relations* 38 (March): 7–48.

Addison, John T. and Paulino Teixeira. 2006. "The Effect of Works Councils on Employment Change." *Industrial Relations* 45 (January): 1–25.

———. 2009. "Are Good Industrial Relations Good for the Economy?" *German Economic Review* 10 (3): 253–269.

Addison, John T., Paulino Teixeira, and Thomas Zwick. 2010. "Works Councils and the Anatomy of Wages." *Industrial and Labor Relations Review* (forthcoming).

Addison, John T. and Joachim Wagner. 1997. "The Impact of German Works Councils on Profitability and Innovation: New Evidence from Micro Data." *Jahrbücher für Nationalökonomie und Statistik* 216 (1): 1–20.

Albert, Michel. 1993. *Capitalism Against Capitalism.* London: Whurr Publishers.

Alchian, Armen A. 1984. "Specificity, Specialization, and Coalitions." *Zeitschrift für die gesamte Staatswissenschaft* 140 (1): 34–49.

Alda, Holger, Stefan Bender, and Hermann Gartner. 2005. "The Linked Employer-Employee Dataset Created from the IAB Establishment Panel and the Process-Produced Data of the IAB (LIAB)." *Schmollers Jahrbuch* 125 (2): 327–336.

Backes-Gellner, Uschi, Bernd Frick, and Dieter Sadowski. 1997. "Codetermination and Personnel Policies of German Firms: The Influence of Works Councils on Turnover and Further Training." *International Journal of Human Resource Management* 8 (June): 328–347.

Baums, Theodor and Bernd Frick. 1998. "Co-determination in Germany: The Impact of Court Decisions on the Market Value of Firms." *Economic Analysis* 1 (2): 143–161.

BDA/BDI. 2004. *Mitbestimmung Modernisieren—Bericht der Kommission Mitbestimmung.* Berlin: Bundesvereinigung der Deutschen Arbeitgeberverbände/ Bundesverband der Deutschen Industrie.

Bellmann, Lutz. 2003. "Betriebliche Flexibilität—das Beispiel der (Re-)Regulierung der Zeitarbeit." Unpublished Paper. Nurnberg: Institut für Arbeitsmarkt- und Berufsforschung.

Bender, Stefan, Anette Haas, and Christoph Klose. 2000. "The IAB Employment Subsample 1975–1995." *Schmollers Jahrbuch* 120 (4): 649–662.

Bellmann, Lutz and Peter Ellguth. 2006. "Verbreitung von Betriebsräten und ihr Einfluss auf die betriebliche Weiterbildung." *Jahrbücher für Nationalökonomie* 226 (5): 487–504.

Bellmann, Lutz and Susanne Kohaut. 1995. "Effektiv- und Tariflöhne in der Bundesrepublik Deutschland: Eine empirische Analyse auf der Basis des IAB-Betriebspanels." In Knut Gerlach and Ronald Schettkat (eds.), *Determinanten der Lohnbildung.* Berlin: Editions Sigma, pp. 72–93.

Bellmann, Lutz, Susanne Kohaut, and Manfred Lahner. 2002. "Das IAB-Betriebspanel—Ansatz, und Analysepotentiale." In Gerhard Kleinhenz (ed.), *IAB-Kompendium Arbeitsmarkt- und Berufsforschung,* Beiträge zur Arbeitsmarkt- und Berufsforschung, 200. Nuremberg: Insitute for Employment Research, pp. 13–20.

Benelli, Guiseppe, Claudio Loderer, and Thomas Lys. 1987. "Labor Participation in Corporate Policy-Making Decisions: West Germany's Experience with Codetermination." *Journal of Business* 60 (October): 553–575.

Biedenkopf Commission. 1970. *Mitbestimmung in Unternehmen: Bericht der Sachverständigenkommission zur Auswertung der bisherigen Einfahrungen bei der Mitbestimmung.* Bonn: Deutscher Bundestag, 6. Wahlperiode (Drucksache VI/334).

———. 2006. *Kommission zur Modernisierung der deutschen Unternehmensmitbestimmung. Bericht der wissenschaftlichen Mitglieder der Kommission (mit Stellungnahmen der Vetreter der Unternekhmen und der Vertreter der Arbeitnehmer).* (Available at http://www.bundesregierung.de/ Content/DE/Artikel/2001-2006/2006/12/Anlagen/2006-12-20-mitbestim mungskommission,property=publicationFile.pdf)

Black, Sandra and Lisa M. Lynch. 2001. "How to Compete: The Impact of Workplace Practices and Information Technology on Productivity." *Review of Economics and Statistics* 83 (August): 434–445.

———. 2004 "What's Driving the New Economy: The Benefits of Workplace Innovation." *Economic Journal* 114 (February): F97–F116.

Boockmann, Bernhard and Roland Vaubel. 2005. "The Theory of Raising Rivals' Costs and Evidence from the International Labor Organization." Unpublished Paper. University of Mannheim.

Boockmann, Bernhard and Tobias Hagen. 2001. "The Use of Flexible Working Contracts in West Germany: Evidence from an Establishment Panel." ZEW Discussion Paper No. 01-03. Mannheim: Zentrum für Europäische Wirtschaftsforschung/Center for European Economic Research.

Brand, Ruth, Vivian Carstensen, Knut Gerlach, and Thomas Klodt. 1996. "The Hanover Panel." Discussion Paper No. 2. University of Hanover.

Brigl-Mathiaβ, Kurt. 1971. "Das Betriebsräteproblem in der Weimarer Republik." In Reinhard Crusius, Guenther Schiefelbein, and Manfred Wilke (eds.), *Die Betriebsräte in der Weimarer Republik*. Berlin: Olle & Wolter.

Brown, Charles and James Medoff. 1978. "Trade Unions in the Production Process." *Journal of Political Economy* 86 (June): 355–378.

Bryson, Alex. 2004a. "Unionism and Workplace Closure in Britain, 1990–1998." *British Journal of Industrial Relations* 42 (June): 283–302.

———. 2004b. "Unions and Employment Growth in British Workplaces during the 1990s: A Panel Analysis." *Scottish Journal of Political Economy* 51 (September): 477–506.

Bryson, Alex and Richard B. Freeman. 2007. *Doing the Right Thing? Does Fair Share Capitalism Improve Workplace Performance?* London: Department of Trade and Industry.

Büchtemann, Christoph F. and Armin Höland. 1989. *Befristete Arbeitsverträge nach dem Beschäftigungsförderungsgesetz*. Bonn: Bundesministerium für Arbeit und Sozialordnung.

Callaghan, Helen J. 2003. "Battle of the Systems or Multi-Level Game? Domestic Sources of Anglo-German Quarrels over EU Takeover Law and Worker Consultation." Paper presented to the 15 Annual Meeting of the Society for the Advancement of Socio-Economics, June 26–28, Aix-en-Provence. (Available at http://www.sase.org/oldsite/conf2003/papers/callaghan_helen.pdf)

———. 2007. "Transnational Employer Lobbying When One Size Does Not Fit All: Anglo-German Wrangles under the UNICE Umbrella, 1970–2003." EUI Working Paper MWP No. 2007/04. Florence: European University Institute, Max Weber Program.

———. 2008. "How Multilevel Governance Affects the Clash of Capitalisms." MPIfG Discussion Paper 08/5. Cologne: Max Planck Institute for the Study of Societies.

Cappelli, Peter and David Neumark. 2005. "Do High-Performance Work Practices Improve Establishment-Level Outcomes?" *Industrial and Labor Relations Review* 74 (July): 737–775.

Carley, Mark. 1998. *Worker Directors. A Comparative Study of Five Countries (Finland, Germany, Greece, Ireland and the Netherlands)*. Düsseldorf: Hans Böckler Stiftung.

Commission. 1989a. "Community Charter of Fundamental Social Rights." COM(89) 471 final. Brussels: Commission of the European Communities.

Commission. 1989b. "Communication from the Commission Concerning Its Action Program Relating to the Implementation of the Community Charter of Basic Social Rights for Workers." COM(89) 568 final. Brussels: Commission of the European Communities.

Commission. 2000. "Communication from the Commission to the Council, the European Parliament, the Economic and Social Committee and the Committee of the Regions. Social Policy Agenda." COM(2000) 379 final. Brussels: Commission of the European Communities.

Cooke, William N. 1994. "Employee Participation Programs: Group-Based Incentives, and Company Performance: A Union-Nonunion Comparison." *Industrial and Labor Relations Review* 47 (July): 594–609.

Dammann, Jens C. "The Future of Codetermination after Centros: Will German Corporate Law Move Closer to the U.S. Model." *Fordham Journal of Corporate and Financial Law* 8: 607–681.

DGB. 2004. "Stellungnahme des DGB Bundesvorstandes, Abt. Mitbestimmung und Rechtpolitik zu dem Bericht der 'Kommission Mitbestimmung' von BDA und BDI." Berlin: Deutscher Gewerkschaftsbund, November.

Dilger, Alexander. 2002. *Ökonomik betrieblicher Mitbestimmung*. Munich and Mering: Rainer Hampp Verlag.

Düll, Herbert and Peter Ellguth. 1999. "Atypische Beschäftigung: Arbeit ohne betriebliche Interessenvertretung." *WSI-Mitteilungen* 52 (3): 165–176.

Dustmann, Christian and Uta Schönberg. 2004. "Training and Union Wages." IZA Discussion Paper No. 1435. Bonn: Institut zur Zukunft der Arbeit/ Institute for the Study of Labor.

Ellguth, Peter. 2005. "Betriebe ohne Betriebsrat—welche Rolle spielen betriebsspezifische Formen der Mitarbeitervertretung?" *Industrielle Beziehungen* 12 (2): 149–177.

———. 2006. "Betriebe ohne Betriebsrat—Verbreitung, Entwicklung und Characteristika—unter Berücksichtigung betriebsspezifischer Formen der Mitarbeitervertretung." In Ingrid Artus, Sabine Böhm, Stefan Lücking, and Rainer Trinczek (eds.), *Betriebe ohne Betriebsrat. Informelle Interessenvertretung in Unternehmen*. Frankfurt and New York: Campus Verlag, pp. 43–80.

Ellguth, Peter and Markus Promberger. 2004. "Arbeitszeitsituation und Betriebsrat—eine Matched-Pair-Analyse mit Daten des IAB-Betriebspanels." In Lutz Bellmann and Claus Schnabel (eds.), *Betriebliche Arbeitszeitpolitik in Wandel*. Beiträge zur Arbeitsmarkt- und Berufsforschung. Nuremberg: Institute for Employment Research, pp. 111–131.

European Court of Justice. 1999. *Centros Ltd. v. Efhvervs-og Selskabsstyrelsen*. Case C-212/97. E.C.R. 1–1459.

European Industrial Relations Review. 2002. "European Company Statute Adopted." *EIRR* 336 (January): 21–25.

Fauver, Larry and Michael E. Fuerst. 2006. "Does Good Corporate Governance Include Employee Representation? Evidence from German Corporate Boards." *Journal of Financial Economics* 82 (December): 673–710.

Feld, Lars P. 2007. "Regulatory Competition and Federalism in Switzerland: Diffusion by Horizontal and Vertical Interaction." In Peter Bernholz and Roland Vaubel (eds.), *Political Competition and Economic Regulation*. London and New York: Routledge, pp. 200–240.

Fischer, Gabriele, Florian Janik, Dana Müller, and Alexandra Schmucker. 2008. "The IAB Establishment Panel—From Sample to Survey to Projection." FDZ Methodenreport No 01/2008. Nuremberg: Institute for Employment Research.

Fitzenberger, Bernd, Karsten Kohn, and Alexander C. Lembcke. 2006. "Union Wage Effects in Germany: Union Density or Collective Bargaining?" Unpublished Paper. Johann Wolfgang Goethe-Universität Frankfurt-am-Main.

———. 2008. "Union Density and Varieties of Coverage: The Anatomy of Union Wage Effects in Germany." IZA Discussion Paper No. 3356. Bonn: Institut zur Zukunft der Arbeit/Institute for the Study of Labor.

FitzRoy, Felix and Kornelius Kraft. 1985. "Unionization, Wages, and Efficiency: Theories and Evidence from the U.S. and West Germany." *Kyklos* 38 (4): 537–554.

FitzRoy, Felix and Kornelius Kraft. 1987a. "Cooperation, Productivity, and Profit Sharing." *Quarterly Journal of Economics* 102 (February): 23–35.

———. 1987b. "Efficiency and Internal Organization: Works Councils in West German Firms." *Economica* 54 (November): 493–504.

———. 1990. "Innovation, Rent-Sharing and the Organization of Labor in the Federal Republic of Germany." *Small Business Economics* 2 (June): 95–103.

———. 1993. "Economic Effects of Codetermination." *Scandinavian Journal of Economics* 95 (September): 365–375.

———. 1995. "On the Choice of Incentives in Firms." *Journal of Economic Behavior and Organization* 26 (January): 145–160.

———. 2005. "Co-determination, Efficiency, and Productivity." *British Journal of Industrial Relations* 43 (June): 233–247.

Freeman Richard B. 1976. "Individual Mobility and Union Voice in the Labor Market." *American Economic Review, Papers and Proceedings* 66 (May): 361–368.

———. 1978. "Job Satisfaction as an Economic Variable." *American Economic Review, Papers and Proceedings* 68 (May): 135–141.

———. 1980. "The Exit-Voice Tradeoff in the Labor Market: Unionism, Job Tenure, Quits and Separations." *Quarterly Journal of Economics* 94 (June): 643–674.

Freeman, Richard B. and Edward P. Lazear. 1995. "An Economic Analysis of Works Councils." In Joel Rogers and Wolfgang Streeck (eds.), *Works Councils: Consultation, Representation and Cooperation in Industrial Relations*. Chicago, IL: University of Chicago Press, pp. 27–52.

Freeman Richard B. and James L. Medoff. 1979. "The Two Faces of Unionism." *Public Interest* 57 (Fall): 69–93.

———. 1983. "The Impact of Collective Bargaining: Can the New Facts Be Explained by Monopoly Unionism?" In Joseph D. Reid, Jr. (ed.), *New Approaches to Labor Unions*. Greenwich, CT: JAI Press, pp. 293–332.

———. 1984. *What Do Unions Do?* New York: Basic Books.

Frege, Carola. 2002. "A Critical Assessment of the Theoretical and Empirical Research on German Works Councils." *British Journal of Industrial Relations* 40 (June): 221–248.

Frick, Bernd. 1996. "Codetermination and Personnel Turnover: The German Experience." *Labour* 10 (2): 407–430.

———. 1997. *Mitbestimmung und Personalfluktuation*. München and Mering: Rainer Hampp Verlag.

———. 2001. "High Performance Practices und betriebliche Mitbestimmung: Komplementär oder substitutiv?—Empirische Befunde für den deutschen Maschinenbau." Wittener Diskussionspapiere, Heft Nr. 88. Universität Witten-Herdecke.

———. 2002a. "Mandated Codetermination, Voluntary Profit Sharing and Firm Performance." Unpublished Paper. University of Witten-Herdecke.

———. 2002b. "Ökonomische Analyse der deutschen Betriebsverfassung." In Dieter Sadowski and Ulrich Walwei (eds.), *Die ökonomische Analyse des Arbeitrechts*. Nürnberg: Bundesanstalt für Arbeit.

———. 2006. "Codetermination and Personnel Turnover: Ten Years Later." *Schmollers Jahrbuch* 126 (2): 287–305.

Frick, Bernd and Dieter Sadowski. 1995. "Works Councils, Unions, and Firm Performance." In Friedrich Buttler, Wolfgang Franz, Ronald Schettkat, and David Soskice (eds.), *Institutional Frameworks and Labor Market Performance*. London and New York: Routledge, pp. 46–81.

Frick, Bernd and Iris Möller. 2003. "Mandated Works Councils and Firm Performance: Labor Productivity and Personnel Turnover in German Establishments." *Schmollers Jahrbuch* 123 (3): 423–454.

Furubotn, Eirik. 1988. "Codetermination and the Modern Theory of the Firm: A Property Rights Approach." *Journal of Business* 61 (April): 165–181.

Gallego, Juan Miguel Gallego. 2007. "Works Councils: An Agency Perspective." Unpublished Paper. GREMAQ, Université de Toulouse 1.

Gerlach, Knut and Gesine Stephan. 2006. "Bargaining Regime and Wage Dispersion." *Jahrbücher für Nationalökonomie und Statistik* 226 (6): 629–649.

Gerlach, Knut, Olaf Hübler, and Wolfgang Meyer. 2002. "Investitionen, Weiterbildung und betriebliche Reorganisation." *Mitteilungen aus der Arbeitsmarkt- und Berufsforschung* 35 (4): 546–565.

Gerlach, Knut, Olaf Hübler, and Wolfgang Meyer. 2003. "The Hannover Firm Panel (HFP)." *Schmollers Jahrbuch* 123 (3): 463–470.

Gerlach, Knut and Uwe Jirjahn. 2001. "Employer Provided Further Training: Evidence from German Establishment Data." *Schmollers Jahrbuch* 121 (2): 139–164.

Gerlach, Knut and Wolfgang Meyer. 2007. "Wage Effects of Works Councils and Collective Agreements in Germany." Unpublished Paper. Leibniz Universität Hannover.

Gorton, Gary and Frank A. Schmid. 2004. "Capital, Labor, and the Firm: A Study of German Codetermination." *Journal of the European Economic Association* 2 (September): 863–905.

Granero, Luis M. 2006. "Codetermination, R&D, and Employment." *Journal of Institutional and Theoretical Economics* 162 (June): 309–328.

Gurdon, Michael A. and Anoop Rai. 1990. "Codetermination and Enterprise Performance: Empirical Evidence from West Germany." *Journal of Economics and Business* 42 (December): 289–302.

Gürtzgen, Nicole. 2004. "Rent Sharing and Collective Wage Contracts— Evidence from German Establishment-Level Data." Unpublished Paper. Mannheim: Zentrum für Europäische Wirtschaftsforschung/Center for European Economic Research.

———. 2009. "Rent-Sharing and Collective Bargaining Coverage—Evidence from Linked Employer-Employee Data." *Scandinavian Journal of Economics* 111 (2): 323–349.

———. 2006 "The Effect of Firm- and Industry-Level Contracts on Wages. Evidence from Longitudinal Linked Employer-Employee Data." ZEW Discussion Paper No. 06-082. Mannheim: Zentrum für Europäische Wirtschaftsforschung/Center for European Economic Research.

Hafner, Hans-Peter. 2005. "Gehalts- und Lohnstrukturerhebung im Produzierenden Gewerbe und im Dienstleistungsbereich 2001." EVAS 62111. Statistische Ämter des Bundes und der Länder—Forschungdatenzentrum der Statistischen Landesämter Standort Wiesbaden.

Hagen, Tobias and Bernhard Boockmann. 2002. "Determinanten der Nachfrage nach befristeten Verträgen, Leiharbeit und freier Mitarbeit. In Lutz Bellmann and Arnd Kölling (eds.), *Betrieblicher Wandel and Fachkräftebedarf.* Beiträge zur Arbeitsmarkt- und Berufsforschung, 257. Nurnberg: Institut für Arbeitsmarkt- und Berufsforschung, pp. 199–231.

Hall, Peter A. and David A. Soskice. 2001. *Varieties of Capitalism: the Institutional Foundations of Comparative Advantage.* New York: Oxford University Press.

Hans Böckler Stiftung. 2005. "TNS Emnid. Die Bevölkerung will Mitbestimmung." *Böckler Impuls* 12/205 (http://www.boeckler. de/32014_36341.html).

———. 2007. "Results of the 'Biedenkopf Commission.' The Government Commission on the Modernization of Employee Board-Level Representation in Germany—An Executive Summary." Düsseldorf: Hans-Böckler Foundation.

Hausman, Jerry A. and William E. Taylor. 1981. "Panel Data and Uobservable Individual Effects." *Econometrica* 49 (November): 1377–1398.

Heinze, Anja and Elke Wolf. 2006. "Gender Earnings Gap in German Firms: The Impact of Firm Characteristics and Institutions." ZEW Discussion Paper

No. 06-020. Mannheim: Zentrum für Europäische Wirtschaftsforschung/ Center for European Economic Research. (Forthcoming in *Journal of Population Economics*.)

Hirsch, Barry T. 1991. *Labor Unions and the Economic Performance of U.S. Firms.* Kalamazoo, MI : W.E. Upjohn Institute for Employment Research.

———. 2004. "What Do Unions Do for Economic Performance?" *Journal of Labor Research* 25 (Summer): 415–455.

Hirschman, Albert O. 1970. *Exit, Voice, and Loyalty.* Cambridge, MA: Harvard University Press.

Hogan, Chad. 2001. "Enforcement of Implicit Employment Contracts through Unionization." *Journal of Labor Economics* 19 (January): 171–195.

Hübler, Olaf. 2003. "Zum Einfluss des Betriebsrates in mittelgroßen Unternehmen auf Investitionen, Löhne, Produktivität und Renten— EmpirischeBefunde." In Nils Goldschmidt (ed.), *WunderbareWirtschaftsWelt— Die New Economy und ihre Herausforderungen.* Baden-Baden: Nomos, pp. 77–94.

Hübler, Olaf and Uwe Jirjahn. 2002. "Arbeitsproduktivität, Reorganisationsmaßnahmen und Betriebsräte." In Lutz Bellmann and Arnd Kölling (eds.), *Betrieblicher Wandel und Fachkräftebedarf.* Beiträge zur Arbeitsmarkt- und Berufsforschung, 257. Nuremberg: Institute for Employment Research, pp. 1–45.

———. 2003. "Works Councils and Collective Bargaining in Germany: The Impact on Productivity and Wages." *Scottish Journal of Political Economy* 50 (September): 471–491.

Hübler, Olaf and Wolfgang Meyer. 2001. "Industrial Relations and the Wage Dispersion within Firms." *Schmollers Jahrbuch* 21 (3): 285–312.

Huselid, Mark A. 1995. "The Impact of Human Resource Management Practices on Turnover, Productivity, and Corporate Financial Performance." *Academy of Management Journal* 38 (June): 635–672.

Ichniowski, Casey. 1990. "Human Resource Management Systems and the Performance of U.S. Manufacturing Businesses." NBER Working Paper No. 3349. Cambridge, MA: National Bureau of Economic Research.

Ichniowski, Casey and Kathryn Shaw. 1995. "Old Dogs and New Tricks: Determinants of the Adoption of Productivity-Enhancing Work Practices." *Brookings Papers on Economic Activity: Microeconomics*, pp. 1–65.

Ichniowski, Casey, Thomas A. Kochan, David I. Levine, Craig Olson, and George Strauss. 1966. "What Works at Work: Overview and Assessment." *Industrial Relations* 35 (July): 299–333.

Jensen, Michael C. and William H. Meckling. 1976. "Theory of the Firm: Managerial Behavior, Agency Costs and Ownership Structure." *Journal of Financial Economics* 3 (October): 305–360.

———. 1979. "Rights and Production Functions: An Application to Labor-Managed Firms and Codetermination." *Journal of Business* 52 (October): 469–506.

Jirjahn, Uwe. 1998. *Effizienzwirkungen von Erfolgsbeteiligung und Partizipation. Eine mikroökonomische Analyse.* Frankfurt and New York: Campus Verlag.

Jirjahn, Uwe. 2003a. "Betriebsräte, Tarifverträge und betriebliches Lohnniveau." *Mitteilungen aus der Arbeitsmarkt- und Berufsforschung* 36 (4): 649–660.

———. 2003b "Executive Incentives, Works Councils, and Firm Performance." *Schmollers Jahrbuch* 123 (3): 397–421.

———. 2008a. "Betriebsräte und Beschäftigungswachstum: Spielt der Spezifikation der Betriebsgröße eine Rolle für den geschätzten Zusammenhang?" *Industrielle Beziehungen* 15 (3): 279–291.

———. 2008b. "Works Councils and Employment Growth in German Establishments." Unpublished Paper. Leibniz Universität Hannover.

Jirjahn, Uwe and Stephen C. Smith. 2006. "What Factors Lead Management to Support or Oppose Employee Participation—With and Without Works Councils? Hypotheses and Evidence from Germany." *Industrial Relations* 45 (October): 650–680.

Kölling, Arnd. 2000. "The IAB Establishment Panel." *Schmollers Jahrbuch* 120 (2): 291–300.

Kölling, Arnd, Claus Schnabel, and Joachim Wagner. 2005. "Establishment Age and Wages: Evidence from German Linked Employer-Employee Data." In Lutz Bellmann, Olaf Hübler, Wolfgang Meyer, and Gesine Stephan (eds.), *Institutionen, Löhne und Beschäftigung*. Nürnberg: Institut für Arbeitsmarkt- und Berufsforschung der Bundesagentur für Arbeit, pp. 81–99.

Kommisssion Mitbestimmung. 1998. *Mitbestimmung und neue Unternehmenskulturen—Bilanz und Pespektiven*. Gütersloh: Verlag Bertelsmann Stiftung. (An English-language summary of the report is available at http://www.bertelsmann-stiftung.de/bst/en/media/ReportAbschluss.pdf)

Kotthoff, Hermann. 1994. *Betriebsräte und Bürgerstatus: Wandel und Kontinuität betrieblicher Interessenvertretung*. Munich and Mering: Rainer Hampp Verlag.

Kraft, Kornelius. 1986. "Exit and Voice in the Labor Market: An Empirical Analysis of Quits." *Journal of Institutional and Theoretical Economics* 142: 697–715.

———. 1998. "The Codetermined Firm in Oligopoly." *Economics Letters* 61 (November): 195–201.

———. 2001. "Codetermination as a Strategic Advantage." *International Journal of Industrial Organization* 19 (March): 543–566.

———. 2006. "On Estimating the Effect of Codetermination on Personnel Turnover." *Schmollers Jahrbuch* 126 (2): 287–305.

Kraft, Kornelius and Jörg Stank. 2004. "Die Auswirkungen der gesetzlichen Mitbestimmung auf die Innovationsaktivitäten deutscher Unternehmen." *Schmollers Jahrbuch* 124 (3): 421–449.

Kraft, Kornelius, Jörg Stank, and Ralf Dewenter. 2003. "Codetermination and Innovation." Unpublished Paper. University of Essen.

Kraft, Kornelius and Maqrija Ugarković. 2006. "Gesetzliche Mitbestimmung und Kapitalrendite (Codetermination and Return on Equity)." *Jahrbücher für Nationalökonomie und Statistik* 226 (5): 588–604.

Kuhn, Peter. 1985. "Union Productivity Effects and Economic Efficiency." *Journal of Labor Research* 6 (Summer): 229–248.

Levine, David I. and Laura D. Tyson. 1990. "Participation, Productivity and the Firm's Environment." In Alan S. Blinder (ed.), *Paying for Productivity: A Look at the Evidence.* Washington, DC: Brookings Institution, pp. 183–237.

Malcomson, James M. 1983. "Trade Unions and Economic Efficiency." *Economic Journal* 93, Supplement (March): 50–65.

Menezes-Filho, Naercio and John Van Reenen. 2003. "Unions and Innovation: A Survey of the Theory and Empirical Evidence." In John T. Addison and Claus Schnabel (eds.), *International Handbook of Trade Unions.* Cheltenham, England, and Northampton, MA: Edward Elgar, pp. 293–294.

Meyer, Wolfgang. 1995a. "Analyse der Bestimmungsfaktoren der 'ubertarifliche Entlohnung.'" In Knut Gerlach and Ronald Schettkat (eds.), *Derterminanten der Lohnbildung.* Berlin: Editions Sigma, pp. 50–71.

———. 1995b. "Tarifbindung—Ein Hemnis auf dem weg zu niedrigeren Lohnkosten?" In Ulrich Schasse and Joachim Wagner (eds.), *Erfolgreiche Produzieren in Niedersachsen.* Hannover: Niedersächsisches Institut für Wirtschaftsforschung, pp. 125–143.

Milgrom, Paul and John Roberts. 1995. "Complementarities and Fit: Strategy, Structure and Organizational Change in Manufacturing." *Journal of Accounting and Economics* 19 (April): 179–208.

Müller-Jentsch, Walther. 1995. "From Collective Voice to Co-management." In Joel Rogers and Wolfgang Streeck (eds.), *Works, Councils: Consultation, Representation, and Cooperation in Industrial Relations.* Chicago, IL: University of Chicago Press, pp. 53–78.

Nationales Reformprogramm Deutschland. "Innovation forcieren—Sicherheit im Wandel fördern—Deutsche Einheit vollenden." (Available at http://www.berlin.de/imperia/md/content/sen-strukturfonds/nationales_reform programm_deutschland.pdf)

Rebérioux, Antoine. 2002. "European Style of Corporate Governance at the Crossroads: The Role of Worker Involvement." *Journal of Common Market Studies* 40 (1): 111–134.

Renaud, Simon. 2007. "Dynamic Efficiency of Supervisory Board Codetermination in Germany." *Labour* 21 (4/5): 689–712.

Ringe, Wolf-Georg. 2007. "The European Company Statute in the Context of Freedom of Establishment." *Journal of Comparative Law Studies* 7 (October): 185–212.

Riordan, Michael and Michael L. Wachter. 1983. "What Do Implicit Contracts Do?" Unpublished Paper. University of Pennsylvania.

Rosen, Sherwin (ed.). 1994. *Implicit Contract Theory.* The International Library of Critical Writings Series. Cheltenham, England, and Northampton, MA: Edward Elgar.

Schank, Thorsten, Claus Schnabel, and Joachim Wagner. 2004. "Works Councils—Sand or Grease in the Operation of German Firms?" *Applied Economics Letters* 11 (February): 159–161.

Schmid, Frank A. and Frank Seger. 1998. "Arbeitnehmermitbestimmung, Allokation von Entscheidungsrechten und Shareholder Value." *Zeitschrift für Betriebswirtschaft* 68 (5): 453–474.

Schmidt, Josef and Widmaier, Ulrich. 1992. *Flexible Arbeitssysteme in Maschinenbau: Ergebnisse aus dem Betriebspanel des Sonderforschungsbereichs 187.* Opladen: Leske & Budrich.

Schnabel, Claus and Joachim Wagner. 1994. "Industrial Relations and Trade Union Effects on Innovation in Germany." *Labour* 8 (3): 489–503.

Schulten, Thorsten and Stefan Zagelmeyer. 1998. "Board-Level Employee Representation in Europe." *EIROnline*, TN:9809201. (Available at http://www.eurofound.europa.eu/eiro/1998/09/study/tn9809201s.htm)

Sommer, Michael. 2006. "Mitbestimmung ausbauen statt abbauen." DGB Press Release, August 30, 2006. (Available at http://www.dgb.de/presse/pressemeldungen/pmdb/pressemeldung_single?pmid=2815)

Stephan, Gesine and Knut Gerlach. 2005. "Wage Settlements and Wage Setting: Results from a Multi-Level Model." *Applied Economics* 37 (November): 2297–2306.

Stettes, Oliver. 2006. "Thirtieth Anniversary of Codetermination Act Celebrated." *EIROnline*, DE0609059I. (Available at http://www.eurofound.europa.eu/eiro/2006/09/articles/de0609059i.htm)

Streeck, Wolfgang. 1992. *Social Institutions and Economic Performance: Studies of Industrial Relations in Advanced Capitalist Economies.* Newbury Park, CA: Sage.

Svejnar, Jan. 1981. "Relative Wage Effects of Unions, Dictatorship and Co-determination: Econometric Evidence from Germany." *Review of Economics and Statistics* 63 (May): 188–197.

———. 1982. "Codetermination and Productivity: Empirical Evidence from the Federal Republic of Germany." In David C. Jones and Jan Svejnar (eds.), *Participatory and Self-Managed Firms.* Lexington, MA: Lexington Books, pp. 199–212.

Thelen, Kathleen A. 1991. *Union of Parts. Labor Politics in Postwar Germany.* Ithaca, NY: Cornell University Press.

Vaubel, Roland. 2007. "Comment—The Strategy of Raising Rivals' Costs by Federal Regulation under Bismarck." In Peter Bernholz and Roland Vaubel (eds.), *Political Competition and Economic Regulation.* London and New York: Routledge, pp. 194–199.

———. 2008. "The Political Economy of Labor Market Regulation by the European Union." *Review of International Organizations* 3 (4): 435–465.

Vitols, Sigurt. 2006. "Ökonomische Auswirkungen der paritätischen Mitbestimmung: Eine ökonomische Analyse. Gutachten im Auftrag des DGB Bundesvorstandes, Bereich Mitbesdstimmung und Unternehmens Politik." (Available at www.boekler.de)

Wagner, Joachim, Thorsten Schank, Claus Schnabel, and John T. Addison. 2006. "Works Councils, Labor Productivity, and Plant Heterogeneity: First Evidence from Quantile Regressions." *Jahrbücher für Nationalökonomie und Statistik* 226 (5): 505–518.

Werner, J Jörg-Richard and Jochen Zimmermann. 2005. "Unternehmerische Mitbestimmung in Deutschland: eine empirische Analyse der Auswirkungen von Gewerkschaftsmacht in Aufsichtsräten." *Industrielle Beziehungen* 12 (3): 339–354.

Wever, Kirsten. 1994. "Learning from Works Councils: Five Unspectacular Cases from Germany." *Industrial Relations* 33 (October): 467–481.

Widmaier, Ulrich. 2001. "The German Mechanical Engineering Industry and the NIFA-Panel." *Schmollers Jahrbuch* 121 (2): 275–284.

Williamson, Oliver E., Michael L. Wachter, and Jeffrey E. Harris. 1975. "Understanding the Employment Relation: The Analysis of Idiosyncratic Exchange." *Bell Journal of Economics* 6 (Spring): 250–278.

Wolf, Elke and Thomas Zwick. 2002. "Reassessing the Impact of High Performance Workplaces." ZEW Discussion Paper No. 02-07. Mannheim: Zentrum für Europäische Wirtschaftsforschung/Center for European Economic Research.

———. 2008. Reassessing the Productivity Impact of Employee Involvement and Financial Incentives." *Schmalensee Business Review* 60 (2): 160–181.

Wood, Stephen and Lilian de Menezes. 1998. "High-Commitment Management in the U.K.: Evidence from the Workplace Industrial Relations Survey and Employers' Manpower and Skills Practices Survey." *Human Relations* 51 (April): 485–515.

Zumbansen, Peer. 2002. Germany Inc. Eroding? Board Structure, CEO and Rhenish Capitalism." *German Law Journal* 3 (June). (Available at http://www.germanlawjournal.com/article.php?id=156)

Zumbansen, Peer and Daniel Saam. 2007. "The ECJ, Volkswagen and European Corporate Law: Reshaping the European Varieties of Capitalism." *German Law Journal* 8 (November): 1027–1051.

Zwick, Thomas. 2004. "Employee Participation and Productivity." *Labor Economics* 11 (6): 715–740.

———. 2005. "Continuing Vocational Training Forms and Establishment Productivity in Germany." *German Economic Review* 6 (2): 155–184.

———. 2006. "The Impact of Training Intensity on Establishment Productivity." *Industrial Relations* 45 (January): 26–46.

Index